Advice for my Granddaughter
For when I'm gone

Robert A. Hall

All author's proceeds from this book will be donated to the
Pulmonary Fibrosis Foundation

D1570924

ISBN-13: 978-1470042387

ISBN-10: 147004238X

Dedication

For Britnye Ruby Vela

Royalties

The author has directed that all his royalties from this book be directed to the Pulmonary Fibrosis Foundation, http://www.pulmonaryfibrosis.org/. (Pulmonary Fibrosis Foundation, 811 W. Evergreen, Suite 204, Chicago, IL 60642.)

The mission of the Pulmonary Fibrosis Foundation (PFF) is to help find a cure for idiopathic pulmonary fibrosis (IPF), advocate for the pulmonary fibrosis community both locally and in Washington, D.C., promote disease awareness, and provide a compassionate environment for patients and their families.

However, the author is solely responsible for all opinion and content in this work. The Pulmonary Fibrosis Foundation has not reviewed or approved the content in any way, and has no responsibility for it. They are noted here only because the author is donating royalties from this book to them.

Acknowledgements

Special thanks go to Britnye's Grandmother, Bonnie Hall, my loving wife, chief cheerleader and tireless proofreader. But I alone am responsible for missed typos, errors and the opinions expressed in this book.

I've written these chapters over several months as I got a spare moment from other demands on my time. I'm sure there is some advice has been repeated in more than one chapter. That just means it is really good advice and you should write it down!

About the Author

Robert A. Hall has been a successful non-profit executive since 1982. Prior to entering that field, Hall served five terms in the Massachusetts State Senate. He was first elected in 1972, the year he graduated from college, defeating a Democrat incumbent by nine votes out of 60,000 cast, in a 4-1 Democrat district, last won by a Republican in 1938. He was re-elected four times by increasing margins, carrying every city and town in the district, and was nominated by both parties in 1976. He was Minority Whip when he retired undefeated in 1982.

Hall holds an Associate's degree in liberal arts from Mount Wachusett Community College (1970), a Bachelor's degree in government from the University of Massachusetts (1972) and a Master's of Education degree in history from Fitchburg State University (1980).

He is also a Marine Vietnam veteran, having served four years in the regulars before college and, while a senator, another six in the reserves, finishing with the rank of Staff Sergeant.

A frequently-published freelance writer, Hall's columns, articles, short stories and poetry have appeared in over 75 local and national publications.

His book of anecdotes about the Marines and politics, *The Good Bits*, was published by www.authorhouse.com in 2005.

His book on association management, *Chaos for Breakfast: Practical Help and Humor for the Non-profit Executive* was published in 2008 by the American Society of Association Executives, www.asaecenter.org. (All royalties go to charity.)

CYA: Protecting Yourself in the Modern Jungle, a humor/self-help book was produced by PublishAmerica in 2010. www.publishamerica.net/product93291.html.

A political book, *The Coming Collapse of the American Republic*, was published by CreateSpace, a subsidiary of Amazon.com, in 2011. http://tiny.cc/g02s4

And *Old Jarhead Poems: The Heart of a Marine* was also published by CreateSpace in 2011. http://tiny.cc/cypoi

All royalties from both these last two books go to *The Injured Marine Semper Fi Fund* to help wounded veterans.

Currently he manages an association, reads extensively and writes articles for his political blog, *The Old Jarhead.* He is a former Scottish Country Dancer, but his Pulmonary Fibrosis curtails physical activities as he requires oxygen for mobility. Comments may be sent to him at tartanmarine@gmail.com.

Table of Contents

Introduction

I was never a father. In fact, I was a bachelor until I married Bonnie when I was 46, in 1992. She was a widow with two teens, but they were uninterested in having me in a father's role and at an age where they were beyond my ability to influence, for good or ill. The efforts I made to be a step-father to them were mostly rejected, my advice spurned, their choices almost universally bad. This produced heartache for my sweet wife which she didn't deserve. If I had a dollar for every tear she shed over them, I'd be wealthy indeed.

So when my step-daughter presented us with a baby in September of 2000, I wasn't particularly interested in becoming a grandfather. The little girl was born into difficult, but unfortunately all-too-common circumstances in 21st century America.

But sometimes God gives you a mission you didn't sign up for. All I had to do was hold Britnye, and I developed a bond of love with her that was as great, certainly, as that of any biological grandfather.

Bonnie and I have done our best to provide Britnye with an island of love, of stability and of, if you will, old fashioned values in a turbulent sea. We have also tried to provide her the material support to have a semblance of a normal, middleclass American childhood, while not having the resources diverted from her to other purposes, or beggaring ourselves in our old age..

Unfortunately, late in 2005 I developed a permanent cough, and was diagnosed with "early interstitial fibrosis" in June of 2006. I have coughed every day since. My mother died of Pulmonary Fibrosis in 1995, and it is believed there is a hereditary component, though the causes are usually unknown. In January 2010, the pulmonologist did a bronchoscopy and determined that I did, indeed, have full blown PF. Since this is an eventually-terminal illness, that's not something to celebrate. In June of 2010 I went on oxygen, so I drag "Oscar the O2 Tank" with me wherever I go.

The doctor originally thought I had Idiopathic Pulmonary Fibrosis (IPF), but now believes I have Non-Specific Interstitial Pneumonitis (NSIP), a less aggressive form of PF, which is good, given that the average time from diagnosis to death with PF is considered to be three to five years, putting me past my "sell-by" date..

At this writing I'm stable, despite the cough and oxygen needs, and still able to work full time. With PF, you can be stable for years. You can also decline suddenly over a period of a few months, and the declines are not reversible. And eventually terminal. Still, at 65, I've had a great life and have lived longer and better than 99% of the people who ever lived, thanks to my great good fortune to be born in the United States, where political and economic freedom, and the protection of property rights, have given even our poorest folks a higher standard of living than much of the world. I have no complaints, and have established a "no-whining" zone in our home.

But it grieves me that I may not be here as Britnye transitions through her teen years into young adulthood, to offer support, guidance and love. So many of today's children never really become independent adults, but remain stuck in perpetual adolescence, dependent on chance, charity and government for support. The world was ever a dangerous place, but it seems the dangers are growing and harder for kids to cope with now.

I fear Britnye may mostly remember me as the old guy who coughed, told bad jokes and pulled an oxygen tank—complete with a bike horn for the little kids—behind him when he walked.

That led me to write the poem below, which in turn led to an essay on my Old Jarhead blog with the same title. I also wrote some advice letters to Britnye, hoping to provide her guidance, since currently I'm in Chicago and she is about three hours away in Wisconsin.

I received enough positive feedback from those efforts that I decided to work on a short book, in hopes that if I'm not here, my words would provide the guidance I no longer could, and might benefit other granddaughters as well. At the very least, the miracle of the written word will convey my endless love to her from beyond the veil.

Advice for my Granddaughter

Britnye Vela, Age 10

January, 2011

The world will break your heart, my girl,
Embrace it anyway.
You were a gift from God to us,
To turn despair away.

Enjoy each day you live, my girl,
For joy was made for you.
We see it in your happy smile
And everything you do.

Now live a life of honor, girl,
Of hope and faith and trust,
For duty's just a word for love,
And doing what you must.

Now live for something great, my girl,
For something more than self,
True happiness in service lies--
That is the only wealth.

Now live a life of learning, girl,
And read a book a week,
For knowledge is the Holy Grail,
You'll never cease to seek.

Now be a friend of truth, my girl,
And judge folk by their deeds,
For empty words are honeyed traps,
And lies are evil's seeds.

Don't live to make us proud, my girl,
But live so you are proud
Of everything you do in life--
And shun the evil crowd.

If reputation's lost, my girl,
Then life is but regrets,
So make your word your bond, my girl,
And always pay your debts.

If God is good to you, my girl,
And children come your way,
Don't pass support to someone else,
But parent every day.

Don't live for just today, my girl,
Or you will soon be bored,
The things in life worth having are
The things you work toward.

We do not wish you riches, girl,
By greed are many wrecked,
Contentment only comes to those
Who live with self respect.

We do not wish you ease, my girl,
Existence free of strife,
But all the joy that's found within
The purpose driven life.

    --Your Grandpa

Advice

My Dearest Britnye,

Advice is easy to give and hard to take. As the old jokes goes, "Free advice is worth the price." I don't expect that you will take all the advice I offer here, all the time. The truth of some of it you will doubtless have to learn from painful experience, which is part of the process of growing up. Good judgment, they say, comes from experience. And experience comes from bad judgment.

Nor can I tell you that I have always followed the advice included in this book. Hard as it is for you to believe, I was once young myself. (I'd say "young and foolish," but that would be redundant.) It is just because parents and grandparents look back on their own follies and mistakes with chagrin that they want to save the children from the pain that comes from learning things the hard way.

You will also hear it said that wise people learn from their mistakes. But really wise people learn from seeing other folk's mistakes, and avoiding them.

I hope to be here a few years yet to offer love, support and, yes, advice. But I hope through this book to give you some guidance after I'm gone to have a happy life and to avoid many of those mistakes that will bring you pain. And at the very least, I hope this book with always remind you of how much I love you, and how much joy you, quite unexpectedly, brought into my life.

Reputation

If you had something that was worth tens or hundreds of thousands of dollars, and was very fragile and easy to break, would you treat it carefully? Of course you would.

A good reputation can be worth far more than that. A bad reputation can ruin your life. But some people are so dumb they don't care about their reputations at all.

Reputations are funny things. Your reputation is the opinion other people have of you, and as such it is going to vary from person to person. Often it depends as much on the other person as they do on you. The bad employee I had to fire is going to have a different (and worse) opinion of me than the good employee I praised and promoted. President Abraham Lincoln said "Character is like a tree and reputation like its shadow. The shadow is what we think of it; the tree is the real thing."

The person who is lazy and didn't work hard in school is going to look at the success I've had in life and think I was lucky. The person who has worked hard to build a successful business, and makes five times as much money as I do, is going to think I'm pretty average.

A lot of people think I'm pretty smart. But I'm sure if I met the brilliant economist, Dr. Thomas Sowell, whose books I like to read, he'd think he had to explain concepts to me in a simple manner so I could understand. (He does that in most of his books, because he's so smart he knows that he has to explain carefully and simply to the rest of us.) So my reputation for intelligence would be different with a person who was much smarter than me.

Since your reputation will depend so much on other people, should you not care about it? Not true—you should care a great deal. People who are envious of us, who have bad characters, who believe evil gossip spread by those who don't like us, or who aren't particularly good at discerning character, may have bad opinions of us.

But we all create our own reputations, the way most people who know us, or know of us, view us. If your reputation is good, then it will greatly benefit you. If most people view you as having a bad reputation, then it will hurt you in a hundred ways. And it will hurt the people around you.

Many things in a person's reputation don't hurt or help that person much. I have a well-deserved reputation as a bad singer, but, unless I'm applying to sing in a band, that probably doesn't hurt me much.

Reputation is all about character. Do you have a good one, or a bad one? Here are some aspects of character that will matter a great deal to your reputation.

Are you honest? If I left you in a room with a lot of money, that I hadn't counted, would it still all be there when I came back? If you steal from a person one time, that person will never fully trust you again. If you steal more than once, they will decide that your reputation as a thief is well-deserved and not trust you at all, ever again.

Do you pay your debts? If you borrow money or a book from someone, do you return it? If you buy something in a store with a credit card, do you pay the bill? (Using a credit card to get stuff and then not paying is no different than going in the store and stealing the same thing and running out. It means that everyone else who has credit cards who pay their debts have to pay more in fees, to make up for the stolen merchandise that some people took and didn't pay for.)

There are companies that track if people pay their debts and give them credit ratings, which tell everyone how trust worthy they are. Your Grandma and I always pay our debts on time, and often early. That means we have a very high credit rating. Because of that, we are able to borrow money when we want to buy a condo or a new car. The bank knows that based on our reputation for paying our debts—our credit rating—they will get paid back.

People with low credit ratings, because they haven't paid their bills as they agreed to pay, can never borrow the money to buy a home or a car, and eventually no one will give them a credit card. That's because people don't lend money to people with a reputation for not paying it back.

A bad credit rating can also stop you from getting a good job. Employers often check the credit ratings of job applicants, especially if the employee will be dealing with money or things that could be stolen or sold. They figure that someone who is in debt a lot and can't pay is more likely to steal from them. Employers check the criminal records for the same reason. No one wants a thief around. A reputation for honesty and for paying your debts means that you will have a better life in the future, because people will trust you.

Do you tell the truth? We've talked about lies before, and it can be a pretty complicated subject. A teenager, caught in a bad lie, once angrily said to me, "Everybody lies!" And the problem is, that's true. I think the judgment lies in the purpose behind the lie. I'd categorize lies as "friendly (or white) lies," "justified lies," and "evil lies." Often, the same exact lie can fall into different categories, depending on the reason for the lie.

Here are some examples. A wife asks her husband, "Do you think I'm fat?" Even if he thinks she's a tad on the plump side, if he's kind he'd probably say, "No, Dear, you're just right for me." But if she asks her doctor, whose job is to look out for her health, he better get the truth across to her, though hopefully in a kinder way than using the word "fat."

If your Grandma asks me where I'm going, I might lie and say, "To meet a friend for a beer." If I'm really going to the mall to buy her birthday president, that's a friendly lie. If I'm meeting a girlfriend for a date because I'm cheating on Grandma, that's an evil lie.

Suppose I see a man run into an alley, and a minute later a mean looking guy with a knife runs up and says, "Which way did he go? I'm going to kill him!" It would be a justified lie to say,

"I didn't see anyone," because I'd be saving a life. On the other hand, if a cop runs up and says, "I'm chasing a thief, did you see him?" and I say "No," it would be an evil lie, because I'd be helping a bad guy get away.

If I know someone is always trying to steal from me or cheat me out of money, telling that person I'm broke is, I believe, a justified lie. On the other hand, if you were hungry and needed food and I lied and said I was broke, it would be an evil lie.

So the purpose of the lie determines the morality of it. I tell Grandma friendly lies all the time, but she still trusts me, because she understands. But if you get a reputation for telling evil lies, no one will believe or trust you. Developing the maturity and the ethical sense to know the difference is important. But it's not always easy.

Are you reliable? Do you do what you say you are going to do? If I promise to take you to the County Fair on Saturday, and then I forget or decide to do something else, I won't have a reputation for reliability with you. On the other hand, if something beyond my control happens, say my car breaks down, or there are bad thunder storms that make it unsafe to go, you are likely to understand and my reputation won't suffer with you.

Are you greedy? Are you self-centered? If someone takes you out to dinner, and you always order the most expensive thing on the menu, or order enough so you get an extra meal to take home, you'll get a reputation for being greedy and they won't want to be around you. If you always have to have your own way about everything, and don't think or care about other people, you will get a reputation for being self-centered, and people won't want to be around you. The sad thing is, people who are greedy and self-centered think everyone is like that, so they often don't realize the bad reputation they have with other people.

I always try to give more than I get. If I'm invited to someone's house for dinner or a party, I bring something. If I'm paying a dinner check with a group, I try to pay more than my share. If I'm with a group of guys, I'm likely to buy them more drinks than they buy me. I don't want a reputation of being cheap, which is another version of being self-centered and greedy.

Are you a hard worker? People want to hire and work with people who do more than their share. I always say that in America, people who aren't too smart, but are honest and hard-working can make a good life for themselves. But people who are stupid, lazy and dishonest have terrible lives—often in prison.

While your reputation is made up of a lot of things that you have no control over (at 5'8" tall, I'll never have a reputation as a good basketball player!), the things I've listed here you can control, and they are the most important things for having a good or bad reputation. A good reputation is more valuable than a million dollars—and having it is up to you.

But you must guard it carefully, and work to preserve it. It takes years to build a good reputation, but only a few evil or thoughtless acts to destroy your reputation forever. President Abraham Lincoln said, "Reputation is like fine china: Once broken it's very hard to repair." As in so much, he was right.

The Secret of Happiness

People search for happiness all their lives, and many never find it. And right here, in this little book, I'm going to tell you the secret of happiness.

Stop looking for it. Really, it's that easy. And that hard.

People who chase after happiness almost never find it. Usually they do so by becoming self-centered and self-indulgent. Such people are never happy. They think they will find happiness by being rich, often working themselves almost to death chasing money. Or worse, becoming dishonest people and stealing or cheating others out of what they have earned. But they are not happy. I've never met a happy thief.

They think they can be happy by feeling good, and they drink too much, or abuse drugs, or smoke, or indulge in promiscuous sex. When it doesn't work, they do it more. And these things make their lives very unhappy.

They try to party and do things that are fun all the time, and soon find that the "fun" isn't fun anymore. It leaves them feeling empty.

So how come all these people chase happiness and never find it?

Because they don't know the secret.

Happiness can't be found. It can only come to you when you are doing other things that are important, and not worrying about finding happiness.

The secret of happiness is to care about something more important than yourself. Unfortunately, you can tell people that, but they don't believe it. Self-centered people try it, but soon go back to thinking they are the center of the universe, that only their wants, desires and needs matter, and they can step on anyone to get them. They go back to their parties or their drugs or their sex or their booze. And thus to being unhappy, which they blame on other people.

It doesn't matter what you care about, that is bigger than you, only that it is worth caring passionately about. Caring about being the prettiest girl in school, or having the cutest boyfriend, or eating the most hotdogs in a contest doesn't count.

Caring passionately about important things more than yourself doesn't mean you never have fun. Before I met your Grandma, I had more than a few girlfriends, and we had a lot of fun. Grandma and I have a good time almost all the time. I've enjoyed parties and dancing and poetry and travel and hiking and reading. I like Scotch and, yes, sometimes I've drunk too much—so the next day I wasn't happy at all! All of these qualify as "fun," and we all need a balance of fun in our lives. But they aren't the kind of things you can care about that will make you happy.

Here are some of the important things I've cared about more than myself. I've cared a lot about my country, and still do, working all I can to protect her and to make her better, so kids like you will have the life of freedom and opportunity in the future that America gave to me. I've cared about the US Marine Corps every day since I joined in August of 1964. Of course, serving in the Marines is one way I tried to help protect my country. You know I volunteered to serve in Vietnam, a war (and was lucky enough to have an easy time of it compared to most Marines). I remember being miserable sometimes in the heat or rain or even cold. I remember being bored sometimes. I remember being scared a few times. But I don't remember being unhappy, because I was serving something larger and more important than myself.

I've been lucky enough to have jobs, first as a state senator and later as an association executive, where the work I did made a difference in people's lives. So I cared about my jobs, and happiness came to me.

I've cared about my family, about my parents and brothers and other relatives. Since I married your Grandma in 1992, I've cared about her more than anything but my country. That is, until Britnye Ruby Vela was born in 2000, and I started caring about you as much as Grandma. Every day, I ask God to protect Grandma and to protect you—and to do whatever he thinks best with me.

Caring passionately about these things more than I have cared about myself have made me a very happy person, though I didn't set out to chase happiness.

Sure, I have bad days when bad things make me unhappy. The car breaks down. Or some lowlife steals from me. Someone does something mean to me at work. But because I have these basic building blocks of happiness in my life—things I care about—I get over being angry or unhappy pretty fast.

There are lots of other things you could care about that would make you just as happy. Working as a volunteer in an organization, or having a job where you help people. Getting involved in your church or other place of worship. Taking care of stray or abused dogs and cats. Getting food for the hungry. It's a long list.

The trick is to have something, or even better several things, you are involved in that are important and that you care about more than yourself.

As I write this, you are eleven-years-old. But Grandma and I have noticed that you tend to be "other-centered," that is, you care a lot about other people, not just yourself. That's a good sign, because you can often spot the self-centered kid by that age. If you turn out that way, you will be happy. People who care about things, like money, are usually unhappy. People who care about other people are usually happy. People who are kind and generous are usually happy. People who are selfish and mean are usually unhappy.

If you don't care about hurting your family and the people who love you by doing drugs or stealing or other self-destructive behaviors, you will make yourself and those who love you very unhappy.

You get to choose. Now that you know the secret, choose wisely.

Contentment

Being contented with what you have and who you are is a great part of being happy. If you are a greedy person, you are never contented, because if you have ten million dollars, you want twenty million dollars. There are always people who are richer, better looking, more talented at something who you can be envious of—and that envy can eat at you like a disease if you let it.

I could wish I had been taller, more athletic, better looking, able to sing or whatever. But I have been very content with the gifts that I have. Instead of worrying about the talents I didn't have, I developed those I did have, like writing. If I sat around wishing I was six foot tall, a star football player and a great singer, it wouldn't get me any of those things, but the discontent would make me unhappy.

Being content, however, isn't the same as being complacent. You can be content with who you are and what you have, and still strive to get a better education, to work hard and get a better job, to improve yourself. The trick is to have balance, to have ambition without being consumed by ambition.

Some people are discontented because they never tried to improve their lives, to get a college degree, to work hard at a job so they could get a better job. The source of their discontent is their own failure to put in the effort to have a better life. There are too many people who are discontented because they expect to be given things other people worked for, like money, clothing and fancy electronics. We say such people have a "sense of entitlement." They feel entitled to things they didn't earn and don't deserve, like a kid who didn't study complaining that you worked hard and got a better grade. "That's not fair!" he says. He should be given the same good grade for not studying that you studied hard for.

Many folk are discontented because they want more, no matter how much they have. More money, more fame, more admiration, more stardom. Only a few very lucky or very hard working and talented people become really rich. Yet even the rich can be discontented if they can't control their desire to have more.

Contentment is a gift you give yourself. But never be content with not doing your best or working hard at something worthwhile, because then you won't be content with the life you make for yourself.

Balance

Almost everyone agrees that's it's important to have "balance" in your life. That includes a balance between work and your career. People who don't put enough focus on work, on developing a career, on doing the best possible job for their employer, find that later in life they are still in the kind of poverty-level burger-flipper jobs that are usually filled by teens or young adults just starting out.

But people who become "workaholics," who spend every minute at the office or answering e-mail and reading reports at home, miss out on a lot of the joy and pleasure of life. We are very fortunate that we live in a modern age where an advanced, free-market economy has given many of us the ability to support nice lifestyles with only a 40- or 50-hour-a-week job. Modern technology has given us the kind of leisure and free time for family and other interests our great-grandparents couldn't dream of having. It wasn't uncommon in the 1890s for people to work six days a week, often twelve or more hours a day.

The "right balance" varies for every individual. If you are partying all the time, having fun, or laying around doing nothing, and put fewer than 40-hours-a-week into work, or work and school combined, you are probably not focused enough on work, and are probably looking at a future of poverty. If you are always at work or doing work-related stuff, 80+ hours a week (exception here for medical school residents!), are always tired, and seldom do fun things or see enough of family and friends, you are likely unbalanced towards work. Eventually, this lack of balance will mean that your work and career will suffer, as well as your health and attitude. This is why some companies require everyone to take their vacation time, to keep them fresh for work.

Teens and young adults are notoriously bad about planning for the future. They live in the here and now, and many act like tomorrow will never come. They are unbalanced towards having a good time now, at the expense of future happiness. They often spend most of their time having fun, and as little as possible on school or career. (Case in point—your Grandpa before age 18 when the Marines changed his attitude!)

They spend every penny they can get their hands on immediately, and often borrow against the future, hardly realizing the bills will come due. Some people never grow up and continue this behavior through their lives. But the future always comes. Then they look around at friends who studied and worked hard, who saved money and didn't go in debt, who didn't get into destructive behavior, and envy their wealth and happiness. "It's not fair!" they say. "They have nice homes and cars. I should too." But they made the bad decisions that put them in that position.

The other extreme is sad too. I recently read about a couple who lived in a run-down house, drove an old wreck of a car and never went out to dinner. When they died, it was discovered they had millions of dollars in cash and antique cars. This is the opposite case; people who saved everything for the future and didn't enjoy their day-to-day lives.

I don't have a magic formula to tell you if you are "unbalanced" too far toward one side or the other. A lot of it seems to depend on the personality traits we either inherit or develop when growing up. All I can tell you is that the happiest people seem to have a good balance between work and personal life, between living for today and living for the future.

If you stay aware of the need for balance, you can examine your life from time to time to see if you are too far one way or the other. If you are, I hope you can take steps to refocus and get back in balance.

Making Decisions

For some people, it seems if it weren't for bad decisions, they wouldn't make any decisions at all. And their sad lives show the results of their poor decisions.

We all make hundreds of decisions every day, a few big, some in the middle, and most small. No one makes the right decision every time. In fact, with many decisions, only you will know if it's the right one. If you choose vanilla ice cream and I pick butter pecan, who was right?

With some decisions, you don't know the results for years. People vote to elect Congressmen who pass laws that may be popular now. But the bad effects of those laws might not be felt for ten or twenty years, long after those politicians are retired. And most of the people who voted for them will never be able to trace the bad results now back to their bad voting decisions ten years ago.

In my job, I have to make decisions. In fact, it's pretty much the main thing they pay me for. I can make one good decision, and earn my pay for a month. Or one bad one, and not be worth what they pay me that day.

I like to think that, since the organizations I've managed have always done well, I usually make pretty good decisions. One of the things I learned is that if you wait until you have all the information you need to make a perfect decision, it will probably be too late. And that not making a decision is a decision as well. (If I ask you what flavor of ice cream you'd like, and you can't decide, the decision is, "no ice cream!")

One of my favorite quotes is from John H. Patterson, who said, "An executive is a man who decides; sometimes he decides right, but always he decides." He should have said "person," because women are executives too, but his point was that making decisions was what an executive's job is all about.

Sometimes you make a decision and it's a good one now, but

time changes it. For almost thirty years, I've had to decide who to hire to work in my office to help me with the tasks that needed to be done. Sometimes I've make a bad decision, the person didn't work out, and I had to replace him or her. That is painful, expensive and means the work wasn't done well while the new person was trained. All because I made a bad decision.

Most of the time, I've been happy with my decisions about hiring people. But organizations change over time, and the job the person was hired for often changes as well. Sometime, what was a good decision becomes a bad one, because the person was right for the old job, but not the new one it has changed into.

In other cases, the person grows into the new job, learns more, and becomes an even more valuable employee. That's a happy outcome for everyone, when a good decision turns into an even better decision later on, as things change.

There are some things that will help you make better decisions.

First, is it a big decision or a little decision? Little decisions tend to be things that are short term, that are easy to change, and that don't really impact your life a lot. Some examples would be what to wear today, what movie to see, or should you watch a movie or read a book. (I vote for the book!) Deciding what to eat for lunch is a small decision—unless, like a lot of people including me, you are trying to lose weight. Then a lot of bad small food decisions can make you sick. Or even dead, because being either too heavy or too thin isn't healthy.

And some things that seem like small decisions can have a big effect. For example, not wearing your seatbelt in a car may seem like a small decision, one you hardly notice. Unless you are in an accident, when it can become the last decision you ever make.

Big decisions are those that are hard to change and those that have a major impact on your life, or the lives of those around you. (Your decisions don't just affect you. If you are a responsible person, you also take into account how they will affect the other people in your life.) I've always thought that people who are depressed and decide to kill themselves by jumping off tall buildings or bridges probably change their minds half way to the ground. But then it's too late, for them and for the people who love them.

Some big decisions are:

- Starting smoking
- Getting a tattoo
- Accepting a job
- Choosing a college
- Getting married
- Having sex (and perhaps a baby)
- Getting involved in illegal drugs
- Committing a crime
- Dropping out of school
- Buying a house
- Getting drunk
- Driving dangerously
- Joining the military

Some of these may seem like small decisions. For example, the decision to start smoking doesn't seem like a big deal to many kids. Years later, when they are dying early from a terrible disease like lung cancer due to tobacco, it turns out it was a huge decision after all.

All of these decisions are either hard to change, can have a huge impact on your life—or both. It's more important to think carefully about all the factors that go into making a big decision.

I can't make these decisions for you. And, while I will certainly have opinions about most of them, now, or in the future (if I'm around to have opinions), you are going to have to make your own decisions and live with how they affect you and the people you love.

I can tell you some ways to make better decisions.

First, are you making the decision, or is someone pressuring you to make the decision? If so, are they doing it for your good, (like, say, your Grandma encouraging you to go to college), or are they doing it for some reason of their own (like other kids urging you to smoke, or do drugs or have sex)? If people are pressuring you to do something for their own reasons, that you are uncomfortable with or know isn't good for you, doing it is probably a very bad decision.

Second, ask yourself WWGMD? (That stands for, "What Would Grand Ma Do.") Other people can't ask your Grandmother, of course, but if anyone looks at the decision and asks themselves what a more experienced person with good judgment who loves them would think they should do, they'll almost always make a better decision. You have Grandma, so ask her!

You can also use, "The Newspaper Rule." If the result of your decision was going to be on the front page of the local newspaper, would it bother you if all your friends and neighbors knew what you had decided? If it's something that would embarrass or shame you for them to know, like stealing something or doing drugs, then it's definitely a bad decision.

Can you take more time making the decision? Big decisions require more thought and a better understanding of the facts, than deciding between a strawberry ice cream cone and a dill pickle for dessert. If you can take more time, take it. Big decisions made on the spur of the moment are often bad decisions.

Talk it over with someone you trust. People who have lived longer have more experience with the kind of decision you face. Don't be afraid to ask for advice. But ask people who have good lives because they have made good decisions. And the judgment of other people your age is likely to be worse than yours—don't depend on them.

Ask yourself, "What is the best possible outcome if I decide to do this?" And then, "What is the worst possible outcome if I decide to do this?" Is the potential upside or good result worth the risk of the downside? Here's a good example. A teenager gets in the front passenger seat of a car and considers not using the seatbelt. What's the potential upside? He could save three seconds and have slightly more freedom of movement. He could get out slightly faster if he needed to. What's the downside? Another car could pull in front of the one he's riding in. There's a bad accident and because he's not wearing a seatbelt, his head goes through the windshield and gets ripped off. (When I was in the Marines, I passed an accident immediately after this had happened. It wasn't pretty.) The potential downside is much worse than the potential upside, making not using the seatbelt a very bad decision.

You are not the only person who has ever made this decision. Look around and see what the results are for other people who have made this decision. What are the health and wealth outcomes for those who have decided one way or the other? You can visit a cancer hospital or a cemetery to see the outcome of decisions to start smoking.

Another good rule is to never make an important or hard-to-change decision when you are tired, or have used alcohol or medications. You can't believe how many thousands of drunk Marines and sailors have woken up with a hangover and an ugly tattoo they don't remember getting, but are stuck with!

Lastly, don't beat yourself up when you make a bad decision. We all do. Resolve to make better decisions in the future and to put things right. Sometimes that's hard—or impossible. It's better, of course, to make good decisions, than to spend the time, tears and effort to recover from bad ones.

Habits

People are ruled by their habits. Without habit, life would get very complicated. Imagine if every morning you had to decide what to do first, what next and so on. Habit does that for us. We develop routines for certain situations as habits, and they carry us through the day, leaving our brains free to consider more important items—like what to have for lunch!

But habits can be good servants or bad masters. Consider.

The person who develops good work habits such as showing up every day, on time, and getting along with coworkers and customers usually has a better income than the person who has a habit of always being late—or not turning up at all. Those people often don't have jobs. (Anyone can become unemployed through bad luck, but there is no use increasing your chances of being poor by having bad work habits.)

Think how other habits can help or hurt you. If you have the good habit of brushing and flossing your teeth morning and night, you are likely to have a pretty smile, to avoid big dental bills and pain, and to have more friends. If you don't, you are likely to have rotten teeth, pain and expensive dental bills. And be lonely.

If you develop the habit of taking a shower every day, you are likely to be clean and healthy, and feel good. If you don't, you are likely to stink, and people, including bosses and boyfriends, won't want to be around you.

If you develop the habit of getting your work done for school or your job before you play or relax, you are more likely to do well in school and to have a good job than people who develop the habit of putting off work until the last minute.

If you develop the habit of keeping your things neat and picked up as you go along, you will save yourself time, you'll enjoy your surroundings and you won't be ashamed to have friends visit.

If you develop the habit of always wearing your seatbelt (as you already have), of not speeding or using your phone when you drive, and of never drinking and driving, you are much less likely to be mangled or killed in a car crash—which would spoil your enjoyment of life!

If you develop the habit of exercising and eating good food instead of junk, you are likely to be healthier, not obese, and to live longer.

Developing good work, health and safety habits will likely increase your life span and make you happier. Developing bad habits in these areas will make you poor, sick and unhappy. Use habits as servants, not as masters. People with bad habits are slaves to their habits.

And, of course, some bad habits, like smoking or using illegal drugs, can kill you. As a beauty queen once said, "If you die, you lose an important part of your life." Duh.

Procrastination, Efficiency and Effectiveness

Before I joined the Marines, I was a procrastinator. That means that you put off doing things you should do until the last minute, or don't do them at all. For example, a kid has homework due Monday, but instead of doing it Friday night, he puts it off until just before bedtime on Sunday, and plays or watches TV instead. Then the work is rushed and poor, or sometimes not done at all, and he gets a bad grade

Everyone procrastinates a bit, but people who do it too much don't do well in school or at work. Or in life. Being a procrastinator was one reason I wasn't as good a student as you are in the fifth grade. The Marines taught me to do the things I needed to do first, then play and have fun later. It's been a good habit. Learn to do the things you have to do first.

There is another penalty to being a procrastinator. The things you should be doing hang over your head and spoil your pleasure in doing the things you want to do. Let's say that I need to load the dishwasher, empty the cat litter and take out the trash. And I have a good book I want to read. I don't really enjoy any of these chores. So instead, I procrastinate and put them off, reading my book instead. But the whole time. I'm aware there are things I should be doing. I'm glancing at my watch, seeing how much time I have to read and still get them done before bedtime. Worrying about the things I'm putting off spoils my enjoyment of reading my book.

Eventually, I have to do them anyway. It would have been better if I had done them first, instead of procrastinating. Then I could have enjoyed my book without thinking about the unpleasant chores I still had to do.

I like the way you like to organize things. People who organize their lives well, so they get their work and chores done without procrastinating, have happy lives. They are more efficient and effective.

People say the difference is that efficiency is doing the thing right, while effectiveness is doing the right thing.

Here's what that means. To be efficient is to do things in a good way or in the best way. It's being well organized. For example, suppose you are going to do homework. First you go up stairs to get your books. Then you go to the basement to get some paper. Then you go back upstairs to get your pencils, and so on. That would be very "inefficient" which means "not efficient." Being efficient would mean you got every thing you needed upstairs in one trip, then everything you needed from the basement, and so on. Being even more efficient would mean keeping all the things you need for homework in the same place, ready to use. So it's like "well organized."

If you have two motors that both do the same amount of work in an hour, but one motor uses less electricity than the other one, the motor that uses less is said to be "more efficient." And you can see that a motor is never perfectly efficient—or it would run with no electricity! So a person is never perfectly efficient either.

If we use the timer on the thermostat to use less heat or air conditioning when we aren't home, that's a more efficient use of electricity, gas and dollars.

How about "effective"? Suppose you have a big homework assignment. So you come home, get out your Garfield comic books which are stacked neatly by your chair, and read them all in order. You might be "efficient" in reading them, but doing so wouldn't be "effective," because it wouldn't be doing anything towards the important goal—getting your homework done. In the example above, efficiently using the thermostat timer is an effective way to save money.

But people who procrastinate are rarely efficient or effective.

Pride

Like many things, pride can be good or bad. The Amish people think that pride is a sin, and thus bad. (Sometimes I think they are proud of not being proud!) But they have a good point about some kinds of pride. Taking pride in wearing fancy clothes or having an expensive car or huge house, or being rich, is a bad kind of pride. We'd call that "vanity."

But I think if Amish people took pride in being honest, or being faithful to their religion, or helping their neighbors, or being good farmers and craftsmen (all things the Amish are known for) that would be a very good kind of pride. In fact, I'm kind of proud to know such good people as the Amish I've met— but I don't think I should tell them that!

You know that your Grandmother and I are interested in genealogy, in finding out who are ancestors were. I've gone so far back that I know where my great, great, great, great, great, great, great, great grandfather, John Hall, is buried on Cape Cod! And being proud of your family is fine—to a point—as long as you don't start thinking it says anything about you. If your great-grandfather was president or a horse thief, that doesn't make you any better or worse a person. If you go back far enough, you had thousands of ancestors. In fact, at the stage when John Hall was my ancestor, so were 1,023 other people. Some of them were probably great, but others had to be bums! I would be foolish to be strutting around bragging about the good ones, and ignoring the bad ones.

The great science fiction author Robert A. Heinlein once wrote, "This sad little lizard told me that he was a brontosaurus on his mother's side. I did not laugh; people who boast of ancestry often have little else to sustain them. Humoring them costs nothing and adds to happiness in a world in which happiness is always in short supply." In other words, looking up his ancestors might have been fun, but they didn't make the lizard a better—or worse—person. Or, lizard.

You should take pride in what you accomplish, in the work you do, in what you create, in how well you serve causes greater than yourself, in how honest and fair you are with others, and in all you do to help other people.

Never be proud of clothes or looks or possessions—that is false pride, and makes you small in the eyes of other people, not larger.

Parents often tell their kids to "make me proud of you." My dad told me that was selfish. He said that instead I should always live so that I was proud of myself.

That's pretty good advice. I believe it's important to take pride in your work, and your efforts. If you live so you are always proud of yourself—for the right reasons—you are living a good life.

Self Esteem

There has been a big movement in our country in recent years to build up kids' self-esteem. That is, to encourage them to think they are special, wonderful and terrific. Perfect in every way.

This is natural with little kids. If a three-year-old gives you a finger painting she did, you say it's beautiful, no matter what it looks like, because you want to be kind and you want the child to feel happy. The same thing is done in the Special Olympics, where kids who have mental challenges compete in sports, and everyone is a winner.

But doing this for kids as they get older does them great harm. They grow up thinking they are so special, that the rules don't apply to them. You see this especially with rich kids, who often get in trouble because there are some rules and laws that apply to everyone. If a rich kid jumps off a cliff, he's going to smash at the bottom, just like the poor kid, because the Law of Gravity doesn't think he's special. Or entitled to special treatment.

Kids think they can do drugs, or smoke, or drink and drive or have risky sex and nothing will happen to them because they are "special." They are always surprised when their bad behavior leads to disaster.

So some kids grow up thinking they don't have to work hard in school, they are "special," so they are entitled to get good grades. And some schools agree and push them through. Then they graduate and can hardly read or do math or know anything about the history or government of their country, and the world doesn't treat them special at all. At work, if they can't do the job, they get fired. The boss won't think they are special if they can't perform.

Some colleges have suffered so much from "grade inflation" trying to give everyone self esteem, that almost everyone gets an A in every course. This cheats the kids who studied hard and learned a lot, because they get the same reward as the lazy kids.

Then they get out in the adult world, and they expect the same salary and rewards as the people who work hard to earn money and build a business. But the truth hurts when the kids who studied and worked have good jobs and the other kids don't.

Recently the TV interviewed a young fellow in Madison who worked for *Noodles and Company*. He thought he should have as much say in running the business, and as much income from it, as the fellow who started with nothing, invested every penny he saved, started *Noodles and Company* first as one restaurant, worked very long hours for many years and built the business, which gives hundreds of people jobs. And it gives those of us who go there good meals at good prices. The "worker" who was interviewed called it "Social Justice." His self esteem was so high, he though he deserved the same results for far less work and risk. People grow up thinking they are "entitled" to things they didn't work for, and are angry when the world doesn't give everything to them.

Grandma and I have been a little guilty of this with you, as we love you so much, we tell you everything you do is wonderful. But you are getting older, and we have to be more honest with you, if you are to grow and become a successful person.

When I wrote my last book, I sent it to four friends to read. They could have built up my "self esteem" by writing back and just saying how great it was. Instead, they went through it, told me what was good and what parts weren't clear, pointed out my mistakes, and gave me suggestions for making it better. They were true friends, and because they were honest with me, I was able to correct a lot of errors and make the book much better.

The fact is no one can really give you self esteem. You have to earn it, like everything else, by doing things that are worthy of being "esteemed." The world is a hard place, and sending ill-prepared kids out into it is going to damage their self esteem more in the long run when the world knocks them down.

It's like being easy on soldiers in training and sending them only half-prepared into a war, because you didn't want to be hard on them. There, many of them die, because the enemy doesn't care about their self esteem. For soldiers, tough training is the kindness.

For kids, preparing them for the real world, by making them earn their self esteem, is the kindness. Because then the esteem they—and others—have for them will be based on real accomplishments, not on lies trying to make them feel good.

You have the potential to do great things, and to be a great person. My wish for you is that you will earn a high level of self esteem by doing good things and by having a good character.

Real friends and Being Popular

Everyone wants to be liked, with the exception of some people with damaged psyches. And, in high school and college, being widely liked means being popular. But being "popular" can be a trap.

After all, the girl who lets herself be used for sex by any boy who asks is wildly popular with boys—for awhile. But they don't really like her, because though they may use her, they don't respect her or admire her.

There are many things more important than being popular. It's more important to be respected. And self-respect is the most important of all. Girls who let themselves be taken advantage of, for sex or anything else, just to be "popular," usually have little self-respect. They have low self-esteem, we would say. I think kids often get into drugs, smoking, sex and stealing because they have low self-esteem. They don't think much of themselves and think everyone else looks down on them, so they want to do things they think are "cool" so other kids will like them. But the things they do give them bad reputations, so they are really very "un-cool," Unfortunately, they often don't figure that out until years later, when they look at their ruined lives and try to find someone to blame it all on.

Friends are one of the special joys in life. It's great to have a lot of friends, but better to have good friends. A good friend is someone you can count on and can trust. A person who lies to you or steals from you or talks bad about you behind your back is not your friend, no matter how nice they are to you in person.

Pick your friends carefully. People who are sunny, funny and joyful will make you that way. People who whine and complain a lot will infect you with that as well. Then you'll find the best people don't want to be your friend, because you make them as miserable as you are with the complaining.

Pick friends who have good habits, who work hard, like

school, reading and learning and can be trusted. Those good qualities will rub off on you.

Pick friends who are honest, intelligent, responsible, compassionate (they put other people first). Pick friends who love their families, who like learning, who have values they believe in. Pick friends who are loyal, who won't talk about you behind your back, or betray you in other ways.

Nothing is more common than people who chose bad friends because they are "fun." They like to party, not work. They would rather have a good time than do the things they are supposed to do around the house, at school or at a job. Life is a big fiesta, one laugh after another. They think people who work and study hard are "boring." Then they wake up when they are 30 or 40 years old and discover that they have poor, sad lives because they wasted them on good times with bad friends who are no longer around, or who have equally sad lives. I like to have a good time too. But I do the things that ensure I have a good life, so I can go on having a good time.

Don't be friends with or hang around with kids who do bad or evil things. You may not intend to steal or do drugs, but they may get caught and you may be swept up in the mix and lose your reputation. Or your life.

There's an old saying, "To have a friend, be a friend." That means if you want good friends who will help you and who you can trust, you must be the same way. That is, if you want to have good friends with the qualities you value in a friend, you must have those qualities too. You must be willing to look out for your friend's best interests. You must be honest and loyal with your friend, as you want him or her to be with you. But having one true friend is more valuable than having hundreds of pals you hang out with.

Of course, there will be people you like to spend time with who will be friends, but not the kind of friends you could call for a ride home at 2:00 am in a snow storm. There's nothing wrong with that, as long as you understand how valuable really good friends are, compared to "hang around with" friends.

Friends are like coins. You can have a treasure chest full of junk foreign coins and old subway tokens that aren't worth enough to buy a Happy Meal at McDonalds. Or you can have one rare gold coin which is worth more than a large, new house.

Better to have one golden friend than a thousand who are really just people you know, not friends you can count on. And when you have a golden friend, be sure you are a golden friend as well.

So it's better to have a few friends you have picked for the right reasons, than many friends. It's better to be friends with good people, than with popular people. Anyone who pressures you to do drugs is not really a friend. Anyone who pressures you to smoke is not really a friend. Anyone who pressures you to have sex because he wants to is not really a friend. Anyone who pressures you to do something dishonest or risky (like drive with kids who are drinking and/or driving wildly) is not really a friend.

A true friend is interested in your best interests, not in using you to have a good time, to be popular or to be cool. Those who do that are sham friends.

Unfortunately, real friends are a lot harder to find than sham friends, than people to just hang out with, than people who just want to have a good time and don't really care if you get hurt.

Friendship doesn't just happen. It has to be built, like love, over time. Friendship is like reputation, very valuable, hard to build and easy to destroy with dishonesty or carelessness. And, as with love, it's very easy to be fooled, because we all want friendship and we all want love, so we overlook the warning signs that suggest someone isn't a true friend. Or a true love.

Friendship, doesn't mean the other person is perfect—no one is. Maybe one friend likes to sleep late and the other likes to be up at dawn going for a run. They are not "perfect" for each other, as each has a "flaw" in the other's eyes. But some imperfections, or the absence of some core values like honesty are deal breakers—you can't be real friends with someone you can't trust or respect, even if you are related to them.

You don't get true friends by being "popular" in the way it's used in school. It's far better that you should be respected and admired. And not for your looks, or how you dress or the stuff you own. That's not admiration—that's envy.

You want to be admired for your honesty, your responsibility, how hard you work, how much you learn and how loyal you are.

And if you are admired for those things, you will find that you have good friends who are real friends.

People who are lazy and who cannot be trusted are never admired. They are rarely liked. Even their parents, who may love them as their children, don't really like them, because they can't trust them. Liking is different from loving.

The good news is that you can make yourself into the kind of person who is admired, trusted and has lots of friends. The bad news is that it's not easy. And it's often not popular. But it's worth more than gold.

How Does It Feel?

This story is from my friend, Dave Hollenbeck, a retired California Highway Patrol Officer and is used with his permission:

One of the earliest lessons that my father taught me on how to live was one morning on the dairy near Glendale. In Arizona, if you grow anything from the soil, you do it with water from reservoirs above Phoenix on the Salt River. By a series of earth rows, you channel the water to spread over the land and irrigate your crop. The water came to you in ditches, and was directed out on to the land.

These ditches were about three feet deep.

We had a pair of Collie dogs. The female had given birth to puppies about a week before. Mother Collie was out near the ditch, leading her brood in single file. I found it great sport to pick up a puppy, throw it in the water, watch it disappear, then reappear and swim out. I had tossed in the fourth puppy, when I felt a force on the collar of my shirt, lifting me up, and then releasing me into the ditch. I went under the water, was thoroughly convinced that I was going to drown, came up, and stood on the bottom so that my head and shoulders were out of the water. My father was there, leaning on his shovel. He looked at me with no emotion on his face and asked, "How does it feel when it happens to you?"

I found that question is one a person should ask themselves frequently.

Fads

We tend to think of fads as silly things people wear, like young boys wearing baggy pants and their baseball caps backwards. Or silly things that people do, like the fad, when my dad was young, of college students swallowing live goldfish. (Yuck!)

Fads are everywhere. Sometimes they are started by a popular movie (I believe the backwards baseball cap is an example). Sometimes they are started by a popular entertainer or political figure. Women often want the same hairstyle as a singer, actress or the president's wife. Boys may want a Mohawk haircut if their favorite sports star has one. Short and long hair on boys goes in and out of fashion, as the fad dies out and a new one starts. Not much harm there, as hairstyles can be changed. The fad of kids wearing their underwear outside their regular clothes died out quickly. (Or I think it has.) For which we should all be thankful!

Right now, wearing jeans with holes in them is a huge fad. People aren't content to get natural holes in jeans; because they want to look cool, they are tearing holes in perfectly good jeans. In fact, you can spend a lot of money buying jeans that are already ripped in the right places. Back in my day, says this old man, we had to wear our jeans for a long time to get holes in them. Then our mothers patched them. Saying this to a young person with ripped jeans just proves how old and out of touch I am. But I'm pretty convinced this fashion is just a fad that will be gone in a few years. We shall see.

Some fads are started by people just to see if they catch on. I've read that the idea of putting a wedge of lime in a Mexican beer was started by a bartender to see if it would catch on. If that's true, he did Corona a favor, because it overtook Heineken as the leading imported beer. And the fad probably wouldn't have caught on if people didn't like the taste.

There is no harm in fads that are just silly. (Though I'm not sure swallowing live goldfish was good for the college boys. It certainly wasn't for the fish.)

Fads can come, go and come back. When I was your age, the Hula Hoop was a huge fad, for a year or two. Then it pretty much died out, but in recent years has made a revival. And you are pretty good at it! (I sure never was.)

Some fads are created by folks who want to make money. Think how many people bought "collectible" Beanie Babies as an "investment" for $15 each, that you can now buy for fifty cents at yard sales.

Fads can also be dangerous, or destructive. Like the current tattoo fad. For the people who regret getting one (about half they say), giving in to the fad can be painful and expensive to try to remove, and can cost them jobs or relationships, if the tattoo was too ugly or prominent.

Fads aren't just about fashion, clothes, tattoos or beer. There are fads in business. Total Quality Management was one about twenty years ago that everyone was trying to emulate, that has mostly faded away. There are fads in education. Schools will group kids of similar ability together (called "homogenous grouping") on the theory that they learn better that way, since they have similar abilities. A few years later the fad is to group kids of varied abilities together (heterogonous grouping), so the slower kids will learn from and emulate the smarter or more hard-working kids. My dad was a teacher for a long time, and he told me this changed several times during his career.

It's often hard to know when something is a valuable new development, or when it's a fad that will be replaced by the next fad in a few months or years. Of course, adopting the fad can be quite costly, especially if it doesn't work well.

As I write, Twitter has been very popular for a year or two, with lots of people signing up for it, and lots of others giving up on it. I don't know yet if it's a fad that will soon fade, or a permanent new way of communicating. (I'm on Twitter, but I'm leaning to "fad." That may be because I'm old and perhaps a curmudgeon.)

When looking at some new fashion, style or behavior that is

suddenly very popular, you should ask yourself a few questions.

Is this a worthwhile new way to dress or behave, or is it just a fad?

If it's a fad, and I get into it, will it hurt anyone, including myself? The stupid fads of glue sniffing and "huffing" (inhaling fumes from cleaning sprays to get high) have killed many kids, leaving the people who loved them in tears for a long time. Clearly they are fads not worth doing. Currently there is a silly fad called "planking," where the kid lays face down and rigid in a weird place and a picture is taken, to post on the Internet. It's usually harmless, but some kids have died because they did it up high, for example on a balcony railing and they fell. Think how sad their families are because of a fad.

If I get into this fad, can I get out of it easily if I don't like it, or things change? (Wearing your hat backwards: Yes. Doing drugs or getting a tattoo: No.)

Will it cost me more money than I can afford?

Will it cost me the respect of people I value, like my boss or my Grandmother?

There's an old proverb that goes something like, "Be not the first to take on the new, nor the last to let go of the old." I don't know who first said it, but it's pretty good advice.

It means, don't rush into something just because it's suddenly popular. But don't be the last person to give up on the old way. After all, people who rode horses to get around thought cars were just a fad.

Courtesy

Back in the wild times on the 1960s—called "the Sixties" by people who think the chaos should be celebrated—one of the things the so-called "counter culture" wanted to do away with was courtesy and politeness. They thought it was phony, useless and a part of outmoded "middle class morality." They couldn't have been more wrong.

People get into conflicts and arguments with each other all the time. They rub against each other and the friction creates emotional heat, just as it gets hot from friction when you rub your hands together rapidly.

Friction can be reduced by grease. That is, if you put oil or grease on two moving parts that come in contact, it reduces friction, heat and wear and tear. That's why you need oil in a car engine. Without it, the heat from the friction would soon destroy the engine. I had a car where the oil pump failed. I didn't know it and was driving down the road when the engine sized up from the metal rubbing on metal without oil. The engine had to be replaced—the old one was ruined.

Courtesy is the "grease" that reduces friction between human beings. That's why Grandma and I are always reminding you to say "please," "thank you," "excuse me," and "you're welcome." (Even though we sometimes forget with each other!)

A very polite person who exhibits a lot of courtesy is usually respected and liked. People say that such a person has "class." And having class is valuable.

Being courteous also avoids conflict. The person who is rude, who butts in line and treats other people with demands rather than "please" and "thank you," gets in fights and arguments—and isn't well liked. Little problems grow into big problems.

Often, in any social situation, the hardest thing to do is the right thing to do. Saying: "I'm sorry. I was wrong. It was my fault." And, "I'll try to fix it" can be very hard. But they are very powerful words, that go a long way to avoiding conflict between people and helping people get along.

People who always have excuses, who try to always find someone else to blame for everything that goes wrong, are not well liked.

On the other hand, people who have the strength of character to admit their mistakes and take responsibility for their actions are respected and admired. It's a wonder more people don't understand that.

Now, if you'll please excuse me, I have to go. I'll try to write more later. Thank you for reading this.

Avoiding Poverty

It's true that there are many happy people who are poor, and many unhappy people who are well-off or even rich. But as the joke goes, "Money can't buy happiness, but it can keep you comfortable and amused while you wait for happiness to come along!"

And grinding poverty, where you cannot pay the bills, or provide the necessities of life for your family, never mind the little amenities that make things pleasant, presents a hard circumstance to be joyful in.

It's also true that many people in this world are poor through no fault of their own. Perhaps they were born into a third-world country where corruption and the lack of respect for property rights means that the development of affluence for most people is impossible. No one invests in starting a business that gives jobs to people if the government is likely to steal the business from you.

Even in our country and the other wealthy democracies, people can be born into situations where the culture, crime and lack of good educational opportunities make climbing out of poverty very hard. And, of course, "poor" is a changing concept. Many of the "poor" in America have air conditioning, cars and more TVs than the middle class did in 1950. I make a good salary, but compared to Bill Gates, or a Hollywood Star or successful professional athlete, I'm "poor." So it can be relative.

Some people become poor because they have a disability or disease that prevents them from becoming successful, or they had a father or mother—perhaps both—die when they were young, making it hard for them to get an education.

But it's also true that many people in our country are poor because they made bad choices. I didn't make up the following rules; I've read variations of them over the years. But if you look at the statistics, there are four ways to avoid poverty:

1. Don't have babies until you are married, your relationship is stable, and you both have good jobs.

2. Get an education, preferably a college education, or at least an education in some marketable skill.

3. Get a full-time job, work at it, and always work full time (that's a 40-hour week) when you can.

4. Manage debt carefully; avoid it when you can.

Absent some terrible event, like a tragic disease, people who follow these four rules may not be rich, but they are seldom poor. Unfortunately, following these rules requires maturity, discipline and good decision making when you are a teen or in your twenties—just when these things are in short supply!

Let's look at these four rules in more detail.

1. Don't have babies until you are married, your relationship is stable, and you both have good jobs.

No factor is more closely aligned with poverty in America than being a single mother. The vast majority of the children in poverty have no father in the house. Sometimes they are fortunate enough to have grandparents who can help the grandkids have something like a normal childhood. But even then, the grandparents get old, and need to save money for their retirement.

Faced with the costs and time commitment of rearing a child, the young father who promised to love and care for you forever when enthusiastically helping you make the baby, often walks away. Trying to support yourself and a baby—or babies—with no help and a limited education is difficult. Yes, the government will take money from the people who earned it (taxes) and give it to the single mothers who didn't earn it, punishing those who made good choices and encouraging more young women to make bad choices. But it's not a lot of money, it doesn't provide much of a life-style for the kids, and as I write, government is fast running out of money.

Yes, sometimes young women marry men without character,

who desert them, putting them in the same circumstances. At least they tried to give their kids a decent life.

The numbers are staggering, especially for minorities in our cities. About 70% of black kids are now born to unmarried mothers. Hispanics and whites are gaining on them. Poverty is more about a culture that leads to bad choices, and government programs that encourage bad choices, than any other factor. In 1950, about 78% of American households were married couples. Now it is down to 48%. Until and unless we can change this culture, we cannot hope to reduce poverty.

The kids grow up without a father in the house, which hurts their development. They also tend to emulate the mother, and have children of their own without being married, passing poverty from generation to generation like a hereditary disease. Single mothers can find lots of dates, but finding a man with a good job who wants to marry them and take on someone else's kids is much harder.

It is my belief that having a baby without being married puts the child at risk. Don't do it to your kids.

2. **Get an education, preferably a college education, or at least an education in some marketable skill**. The last time I checked, the average lifetime earnings was over a million dollars higher for those with college educations as for those with just a high school diploma. Those folks who don't graduate from high school are in very bad shape, and it's getting worse. And even in the recent recession, the unemployment rate was much lower for those with a college degree than for those without one.

And when you go get that education, look at how many jobs there are and income levels of people with degrees like the one you want. There is a bitter joke among parents, that goes, "If your kid is majoring in something that ends in 'studies,' don't turn her bedroom into a den. She's coming home after college, because she won't be able to support herself."

There are a lot of popular subjects to study that are fads. Academics—whose own income is protected by tenure—are happy to teach these subjects, and the colleges are happy to take the money the students borrowed to go there. The future employability of their students seems to be no concern of theirs. When you are ready for college, do some research on what fields have the best job opportunities. As I write, social work, education and architecture are among the worst, but this may change. If there are five people with social work or education degrees for every job opening, four of them are going to be unemployed, or working at something else.

It should go without saying, but I'll say it anyway. Postpone having babies not only until after marriage, but until after you get your education. One of the saddest and most common stories is the young couple who are in love. They get married—or just live together—and decide that he will go to school while she works long hours at bad jobs to support them. Once he gets his degree and establishes a professional career, his waitress wife with two babies no longer seems a suitable partner. He divorces her—if they bothered to get married in the first place—and leave her in poverty, with some child support if she is lucky. He has a good job, a new wife who is well employed, and a nice house and car. The ex-wife and kids live in a crummy apartment. Getting an education and getting out of poverty is now ten times as hard.

None of the tens of thousands of women to whom this has happened would have believed it if you had told them on their wedding day. "He's not like that," they'd have said. "We're in love." If he really loves you, he'll wait until you get your degree. If he doesn't wait—you dodged a bullet.

3. **Get a full-time job, work at it, and always work full time (that's at least a 40-hour week) when you can.**

Many teens get in the habit of working a part time job here for a few months, another there for the summer, and living off their parents. Unfortunately, some never break the habit and carry it with them into their twenties and thirties. Unless they inherit money or win the lottery, they are always poor.

Working full time, no matter how bad the job, gives you a work record, references and job skills that you can take with you to the next job. It brings in more money than working part time, and usually has benefits, which is an important, though often over-looked part of your income. It makes you more attractive to future employers. And it lets you build up a network of contacts who will help you get better jobs down the road.

And don't hop around from job to job. I've been the hiring manager in my office for 38 years, so I've looked at a lot of resumes. When I see one where the applicant had five jobs in seven years, nine months here, sixteen months there, and so on, that resume goes into the "do not bother calling" pile.

4. **Manage debt carefully; avoid it when you can.**
Debt is very tempting. It think it's unconscionable that credit card companies push credit cards on college kids. They are too inexperienced to understand that a few thousand dollars of debt, to buy that nice stereo or new beach clothes, can take twenty years to pay off at minimum monthly payments and cost ten thousand dollars in interest payments.

I didn't have a credit card when I was in college. I paid cash or did without. That may not be practical in today's world, but I recommend it. If you have to have a credit card, make sure you don't use it for more than you can pay off every month. Interest payments on credit cards are high. They help the bankers have nice life styles, but do nothing for you but make you poor.

Many kids run up debt so high they just default. That is, they don't pay. That sticks the banks with the lost money, but they get it back by charging higher rates to those who do pay to make it up. So when someone defaults on a credit card, they are really stealing money from everyone else who has a credit card, and who pays the bills.

Bad use of credit, such as defaulting on payments, or even being late on payments, also gives you a bad credit rating.

Having a good credit rating helps you avoid poverty, for several reasons. First, it helps you borrow money when you do need it, for something big, like a house or a car. Your Grandmother and I have a credit rating over 800, which is very good. It means we can be trusted to lend money to, because we always pay our bills on time—or often in advance. So when we wanted to buy our condo in the Chicago area in 2009, in the midst of the credit crunch, we were able to borrow the money.

As I said earlier, having a bad credit rating also hurts your chances of getting a good job. Employers check them to see if employees are trustworthy. People who are behind on their bills or over their heads in debt are not the people you want in your organization, especially handling money, because they are more likely to get desperate and steal from you.

So being poor often means people misuse credit, get bad credit ratings, can't get better jobs—and get even poorer.

Just because someone will lend you money doesn't mean you should borrow it. A lot of people bought the biggest house they could get a mortgage on, paying only the minimum every month. Then when the housing market collapsed in 2007, they ended up owing more than their houses were worth. The saying is, their mortgages were "under water." They were drowning in debt.

My dad was a school teacher, who worked two jobs to support the family. All the college support he could provide was a roof over my head, and food—if I was there at meal time. Yet I came out of college with my degree and no debt. I had the GI bill, which folks said made me "lucky." But I didn't notice any of them behind me at the Marine recruiter trying to get "lucky" by going to Vietnam with me. I went to state schools, which were cheaper (then), and have been well enough employed since to pay it all back and more to the states I've lived in through my taxes. And I worked 20 to 36 hours per week in college, which carrying a full load—or more—of credits and a good GPA. Debt is a killer.

One of the reasons your Grandma and I aren't poor, is that we always settled for smaller houses and cheaper cars than we could afford, and we paid more than the minimum payments, so we'd get ahead. We also don't charge more on our credit cards than we can pay every month, so we don't have interest payments making us poor.

As I write this, we owe only one debt, $98,000 on the condo we bought two years ago for $160,000. We put $16,000 down and paid off more over three years. With that kind of payments, we could have had a much larger and nicer condo, paying twice the mortgage, but we would have put ourselves at risk of being poor if something went wrong.

Following these four rules takes discipline and maturity, but they will help you avoid being poor. You must be willing to settle for less than you want, less than you can get right now, for having a more comfortable lifestyle in the future.

Paying for a Good Education

It's really important for you to get very good grades in school. I know you want to go to college to be a teacher. Even if you change your mind on that—it happens—people who go to college and get a degree almost always get better jobs and make more money than those who don't. Since almost everyone has to work to live, I'd rather be working at a job I enjoy that pays well, so I can live comfortably. If I hadn't gone to college, we wouldn't have the money for things like the vacations to Disney World you enjoyed.

One of the secrets to getting good grades, by the way, is to always sit in the front of the classroom (if they don't assign seats). Students in the front naturally pay better attention, learn more, are known by the teacher and do better on tests. And it costs nothing extra to sit in front.

But paying for college is expensive. And by the time you go, Grandma and I will be retired and won't have money to pay for it, so you will have to pay for your own college. There are two good ways to go. One is to be so smart and to work so hard in grade school and high school that you get a scholarship, and go to college mostly free. You are smart enough to get good grades, but it takes hard work too. I was always smart, but I was lazy and instead of threes and fours, I got twos and ones! (In those days, they called them Ds and Fs!)

The other way is to join the military, like the Navy, Air force, Army, Coast Guard or Marines for four years, and save money for college. Plus they give you extra money, called the "G. I. Bill," to go to college after you get out of the service in four years. That's how I paid for college. It was also a big help to me to be four years older than my classmates, because I was more mature, had discipline and worked harder. So in college I got As and Bs. Too bad I didn't start sooner—I could have had good grades in high school and gone to a better college. You remember meeting Julie, the woman who used to work with me, Sophia and Theo's mom?

She is a great worker because she was in the Air Force for four years and learned how to be a good worker. And despite being a mom and working at her job, she got her college degree on line at night—that takes discipline, which she learned in the military.

The military will also teach you things. Some people are able to come out of the service and use their military training to get a very good job, without more education. You will also meet people from all over, and from many different backgrounds. That's a valuable education in itself.

Of course, the best reason to join the military is to serve and protect our great country. You know that I served in the Marines. Other than you, there is nothing in my life I'm as proud of as being a Marine. And because of the discipline they gave me and the pride and work ethic they instilled in me, I've had a very successful and happy life.

Of course, the military is smaller now, so they don't take people who aren't smart, or people who have been in trouble with the law.

As with so much, you will have to make your own decision about this. Your Grandma and I will love you and be proud of you regardless. But serving in the military will make you a better person and you'll be proud of yourself. I hope you'll think about it.

Being Cheap or Being Frugal

Some people might not think so, but there is a big difference between being cheap and being frugal. Your Grandma and I are not cheap. But we are frugal. Here's the difference.

Being cheap is not giving your fair share or not sharing with others. Suppose someone invites us to a party or to their home for dinner. We always take something with us. Perhaps it's a bottle of wine or a dessert to go with dinner. Of if it's a party, some beer and chips for everyone. We don't want to show up empty handed and look cheap. We'd rather give more than our share than be thought cheap.

If a waitress or waiter does a pretty good job for us at dinner, we always give her or him a good tip. The way things are set up, some people have to depend on tips for a good part of their income. It doesn't matter if I think it shouldn't be that way, that's the way it is. To "stiff" the waitress (not give a tip, or give too small a tip) is cheap and mean.

Some people are sponges—that is, they always try to get other people to pay for things for them. If they go out to eat, they always let the other person pay. They are always "borrowing" things, like cigarettes or food, that they never repay. They are cheap. When he was in college, my dad had a friend, Ike, who was a sponge. Dad, Uncle Frank and Ike would go into a bar. My dad would buy three beers for them. Then Uncle Frank would buy three beers. Then, when they were gone, Ike would say, "Well, guys, that's enough for me!" So he avoided paying anything, though he drank two beers. He was cheap. They used to laugh about it, but no one really admires a sponge. Try to give more than your fair share.

Being frugal is a different thing. Your Grandma and I try to save money when we can. Because of work, we eat out a lot, but usually at lower-cost family restaurants. We turn the heat down and the lights off when we are not home. We take good care of our cars, spending money to keep them running well, so we won't have the much bigger cost of buying a new car soon. Some people drive their cars hard, bang them up and don't do the basic things like change the oil. Because they don't take care of their cars, they usually drive old wrecks and have higher car expenses.

We both like to find bargains, and shop at Goodwill or yard sales and flea markets (which makes you groan). Of course, we think it's fun to find bargains, so it's not just being frugal. And now we can say we are being "green" and saving the environment by recycling. But really we are mostly being frugal.

You see, it doesn't matter if you are poor or very well off. You still have only so many dollars. If you waste a dollar on the electric bill, that's a dollar you don't have to spend on other things. If I buy a nice sport shirt at Goodwill for $4 instead of paying $20 for it at a regular store, that's $16 I have in my pocket to save for retirement, go out to dinner or spend on my Granddaughter! It may be only $16, but those little savings add up to a lot of money over time.

Of course, you can also waste money by buying things you don't need, just because they are a bargain. That's where I have to be careful—I'm sure I have more four-dollar shirts in my closet than I really need.

If you learn to save money by taking care of things so they last, by not wasting it, for example by leaving a lot of lights on when you go out, and by not spending too much on things that you don't need, you will have a more comfortable life. Money really can't buy happiness, but a lack of money for basic comforts like shelter, clothing and food makes life pretty miserable.

And when you start earning your own money, make sure you have the discipline to save some from every paycheck. As that wise Founding Father, Benjamin Franklin said, "A penny saved is a penny earned." That is, if you save $10 instead of wasting it, it's just as good as going out and working to earn $10.

A last thought. It's good to be generous, not cheap, with those who are really in need. But it's also good to be frugal, not generous, with sponges who should be earning their own money, but would rather talk you out of yours than go out and work for it themselves. And it's a wise person who can usually tell the difference.

Driving Cars

Few things excite a teenager as much as getting a driver's license. It is, as they say, a "rite of passage" in our society. It marks the start of adulthood. It's the opportunity for a kind of independence that didn't exist back before the automobile, when most kids lived on farms and it was often a long walk into town. It's the chance to get a job on your own. Driving is fun, even if you are only driving around your town.

And few things frighten the teen's parents and grandparents as much as that new driver's license. Why the different viewpoints on this major milestone?

Currently, the annual death toll in car accidents is around 32,000. That number has been dropping, due to safer cars, better enforcement of drunk driving laws, seatbelt use and other factors. But a dropping number will be no comfort to your family if you are one of the 32,000 dead this year or next year. Despite the decline in deaths, you still have a lot better chance of being killed in a car wreck then you do of winning the lottery. Sad, I know, but there it is.

A website entitled Teen Car Accidents (www.car-accidents. com/teen-car-accidents.html) says: "Each Year over 5,000 teens ages 16 to 20 Die due to Fatal injuries caused (by) Car accidents. About 400,000 drivers age 16 to 20 will be seriously injured. The risk of being involved in a car accident (is) the highest for drivers aged 16- to 19-year-old than it is for any other age group. For each mile driven, teen drivers ages 16 to 19 are about four times more likely than other drivers to crash." The risk is even higher in the first year the teen is driving, because of lack of experience. And having other kids in the car increases the risk, as the driver is more likely to be distracted, to drive recklessly to show off, or to clown around.

That's why some states have wisely adopted graduated licensing. New teen drivers must have an adult driver with them for a period of time, can't drive with other kids in the car, and/

or are limited in the hours they drive. Such rules cut down on the number of weeping parents burying dead children.

Every one of those 5,000 dead kids last year didn't think it could happen to her or to him. That may be why teens are less likely to use seatbelts than older drivers.

The only good news for you is that boys are more likely to crash than girls, I guess because they like to show off and drive faster, drive without seatbelts and drink and drive. Of course, even that doesn't help you if you are riding in a car with a boy at the wheel.

Everyone alive is at risk of dying every minute. An airplane could fall out of the sky on you—it's rare, but it happens. The trick is to do everything you can to reduce your risk, just like smart soldiers in a war dig a fox hole to hide in every time they stop moving, just in case.

You cannot completely eliminate your risk of dying in a car wreck. You can be the safest driver in the world, and some drunk in a truck can crash into you. I've been in five accidents in my life (so far), all because the other driver made a mistake. Lucky no one was hurt badly in any of them.

You can, however, greatly reduce your risk of dying in a car crash, if you follow some simple rules.

1. **Never speed**. Never ride with someone who speeds. Yes, any driver can get careless, especially in a low speed zone, and exceed the limits. Grandma and I have had speeding tickets. It's especially hard to remember in the 25-mile-an-hour neighborhoods, where the limit is for the safety of kids who may be playing in or near the street, not for the driver, and it feels like you are creeping along. But you wouldn't want to live your life knowing you had killed a child by speeding. And high speed is a factor in a large number of fatal car crashes.

2. **Always wear your seatbelts**. Require anyone who rides with you to wear them. While it's not true that a cop has "never unbuckled a dead person," a lot more of the people killed in car

wrecks aren't wearing seat belts than are. Lack of seat belts is another a big factor in crashes where people die.

3. **Never drink and drive**. Never ride with a driver who has been drinking, smoking pot or doing drugs. Impaired drivers account for a large number of crashes. They have done tests where they have a driver do an obstacle course in traffic cones. Then they have him drink a couple of beers and do the course again. The drinking driver always does worse, but often thinks he is doing better! That lack of judgment makes the risk worse.

4. **Don't let yourself be distracted by talking on a cell phone (even hands free) or, worse, texting while driving**. Don't ride with someone who does. There are studies that say the distraction of cell phones make you drive as badly as someone who has been drinking. Near where we lived in New Jersey, a four-year-old girl was killed by a driver on a cell phone who wasn't paying attention and slammed into her mother's van. Imagine him having to look in the mirror every morning knowing he killed a little girl because he thought his call was so important.

5. **Don't drive if you are tired**. Pull over and take a nap, or get someone else to drive. Fatigue causes a lot of accidents too. We had a neighbor in Madison who fell asleep at the wheel one morning. He died. So did the mother and little boy he hit head on.

6. **Try to only drive or ride in safe cars**. That can cost money, but funerals are expensive, too. Make sure the breaks, tires and other safety features are well maintained. A newer car with safety features like airbags is better. A larger car may not be "cool," but it's safer. Being dead doesn't make you popular either.

It's hard to tell a friend, especially a boyfriend, that you won't ride with him because he speeds, or drinks or drives carelessly or has an unsafe car (or, maybe, all four!). It can hurt if he (or she) gets mad or teases you about it. But having your head go through a windshield at 80-miles-per hour can hurt a lot worse. Having your face scared for life in a car wreck will hurt for life.

7. **If it's raining hard, and you come to a large puddle—a flooded section of the road—don't try to drive through it**. The water can rise very rapidly, stalling out your car, leaving you to wade out looking stupid while you car gets ruined from flood waters. Yes, I know from experience.

Looking stupid and a ruined car are not the worst things that can happen. Every year, some people are in stalled cars in a flood, get out and are swept away and drowned. Talk about wrecking your weekend.

Of course, rain, ice and snow are likely to cause crashes, and require extra care when driving. "Extra care" can be taken by not driving in them at all, unless absolutely necessary.

Nothing can remove all risk of car accidents. But if you follow these rules, you are much more likely to live to an age to worry about your own kids or grandkids driving their first car. (Maybe by then the cars will fly and you'll be twice as worried.)

Bikes, Boats and Other Vehicles

The risk of being killed or injured in a car wreck applies if you are on a bike, a boat, a motorcycle, a four-wheeler in the woods— or a horse. Except that you are more exposed on these modes of transportation, without a large car wrapped around you. Motorcycles and four-wheelers go as fast as cars. While bikes (and horses) don't, they can still expose you to danger—especially to being hit by a car if you are careless. Or the car driver is careless. If you are on a bike and get hit by a car, it doesn't matter who was right, it's likely that you will be the person who is dead. You need to follow all the safety rules above that apply, substituting a helmet for a seat belt on bikes, horses and motorcycles. If you ride with someone else on a motorcycle, you need to be absolutely sure that person is not a clown or a cowboy who likes to show off. 630 bicyclists died on US roads in 2009. 74 were kids 14 or younger. About 4,300 people died on motorcycles in 2011. That's like your whole school being killed.

Bikes and motorcycles are hard to see, and often get hit by elderly drivers (like Grandma and me) who don't notice them and pull out into traffic. Guess who dies? Not the elderly driver.

Try to ride your bike mostly where there is little car traffic, not on busy roads. Always stay alert for cars and other dangers.

As to motorcycles, my dad drove one, but I never did, except to ride on his as a kid. I figured they are too dangerous. Best to avoid them if you can, but always wear a helmet if you do ride on one. When you are flying through the air at 60 miles and hour, about to hit a tree face first, it's too late to remember what Grandpa said!

As to boats, they too cause a lot of pain every year because of careless people. Never go out if the weather is bad. Never go out if the person or persons in charge have been drinking. Never go out in a boat that doesn't seem safe, or without emergency equipment like life vests. No, we don't want you to stay home all the time, locked in the house. We want you to have fun, and to stay safe, so the fun doesn't turn ugly—and there's a next time to have fun. I don't know for sure, but the young folks who got careless and ended up in cemeteries at an early age don't seem to be having a lot of fun.

Taking Care of Yourself

Ralph Waldo Emerson said, "The first wealth is health." By that, he meant that being healthy is far better than being rich. A very sick, rich person, who is perhaps dying, would trade all the money and other stuff he owns to be healthy. And no healthy person would trade with him, even if they could. If you are debilitated by illness and can't do things, you lose a big part of what makes life enjoyable. If you are in pain or feel sick or weak all the time, it's hard to enjoy the best parts of life.

As you know, I used to love Scottish Country Dancing. But I had to stop, first because my feet started hurting too much. Then my lungs went bad with pulmonary fibrosis, so I had to go on oxygen to be able to walk around, never mind dance. That means there are a lot of things I enjoy, likely hiking in the mountains, which I can no longer do. I'd trade a lot of money to have healthy lungs again!

My PF is probably hereditary, not from something I've done. But a lot of people ruin their lungs, or heart or brain or other vital parts by doing things that are bad for them. They smoke. They drink too much. They do drugs. They engage in all kinds of risky behavior. They eat too much, especially of the wrong things.

As you can tell by looking at me, I haven't always had the best diet, or the best exercise program. On the other hand, my lungs aside, I'm in a lot better shape than many folks my age, because I tried to watch my diet and to do at least some exercise.

I don't want you to miss every pleasure in life. You don't have to pass up every ice cream cone now, or every glass of wine when you get older. You just can't overdo it with them, if you want to live a long and happy life. It's harder to be happy when you are very sick, though some people manage.

Exercise is very important. It's good that you love dance class, but you need more than that. Too many kids today spend far too much time in front of the TV or the computer, letting their muscles dissolve into jelly. (And not doing their brains much good either!) Exercise can be boring, so you need to find things you like to do, like dance and biking. Walking is great exercise. So is a sport like soccer. If you develop the habit of getting enough exercise now, it will help keep you happy and healthy all your life.

There are other ways you can protect yourself. We've talked about safety while driving. Many of the same rules apply to other fun activities, like boating. Grandma and I love to canoe. But we never go out without safety flotation pillows. If we were going in deep or rough water, we'd wear life vests, just in case. And we'd never go boating if we'd been drinking. All it takes it one careless moment, and life is over. Often, it can be someone else who is careless, who costs you your life.

In the Marines there is a term, "situational awareness." That means you should always be aware of what is happening around you. Some people become so lost in thought, or conversation or text messages, they don't notice trouble approaching until it's too late. Trouble might be a bad thunderstorm, an out-of-control truck, a train you don't notice as you cross the tracks while texting—or a thug or gang headed you way, intent on hurting you. It happens.

Likewise, you want to be careful where you go, both in foreign countries and in our own country. Some areas are thick with thugs, who would rob, beat and yes, rape you if they got the chance. Night is the most dangerous, as the evil people come out then. They don't want to be spotted in their crimes, so they prefer to operate in the dark. People worry about snakes and spiders and sharks and alligators and wolves. But by far the most dangerous critter on earth, the one that hurts the most people, is the human being.

When you go someplace, let people who love you know where you are going. Grandma and I almost always know where each other are—it's just common sense. Until you are grown, make sure you go with a trusted adult. Be careful of strangers, even when you are an adult. You don't know if you can trust them. There are millions of good people in this world. But there are millions of evil ones as well.

If you go into a strange location, even as an adult, go with someone else. Two people can take better care of themselves than one. Stay in groups. Go to safe, lighted, known areas, like malls.

And be careful on-line, in chat-rooms or social networking sites. Don't give out personal information, like your full name, address or phone number. Be aware that the person you are chatting, texting or e-mails may be pretending to be a 12-year-old girl, but might really be a 40-year-old man with bad intentions. The Internet is a lot like a city, with great areas, a shopping district—and some bad and dangerous neighborhoods, complete with criminals. Take care on line just as you would out in a strange city.

People who are scared of everything are called "paranoid." But being at least a little paranoid can save you from great harm. The old joke is that even paranoids have enemies. I'm not paranoid—or I don't think so. As a Marine, I think I can look out for myself. But there are many areas of Chicago I would never go to. There are even more areas where I wouldn't go at night. And some places or times I wouldn't go alone. It's not paranoia, it's common sense to know the difference between a safe place and a dangerous place.

People who love you, like your Grandma and I, will try to take care of you. But it's mostly something you have to be smart and disciplined enough to do for yourself. And few things are more important to your happiness.

Protecting Yourself from Fraud, Scams and Thieves

The world is, unfortunately, full of people who will see you the way a hawk sees a mouse. As lunch. It's nice to trust people, but you want to do your best to be sure they deserve your trust before you do. One of the more cynical rules for this is, "Believe nothing that people say. Believe everything that people do." What that means is that people lie, often convincingly, and you can better judge them by their actions than their words.

A person who lies to you about important things is not a good person, and cannot be trusted. A person who steals from you, regardless of the reason, is not a good person, and cannot be trusted. My friend, Gene Duncan, had a good saying, "Never give a bum a third chance." What he meant was that anyone could make a mistake and deserved a second chance. But if you gave them one, and they lied, abused or stole from you again, forget it, they were just not good people and you'd be a fool to trust them again. Sometimes you have to associate with evil people who lie and steal for reasons beyond your control, such as at work or school, but try to avoid them as much as you can. They don't deserve to be around you, and you don't deserve to have them abuse you. And people will think you are evil if you hang around with evil people.

Be very suspicious of people you don't know at all. There are endless sad stories of woman sending money to scam artists they met over the Internet, who sold them a bill of goods about loving them. (They never saw the money again.) There is something called the Nigerian Scam, because it originated in that country, but now can come from anywhere. In the old days it came by letter, but now by e-mail. The person pretends to have millions of dollars in some bank account they need to get out of their country, and if you'll take it for them they will share it with you, making you rich. Of course, there is no money (and if there were, it would be dishonest of you to take it). Once they have you hooked, they tell you they need money from you for export fees, or bribes, or whatever. You wouldn't think people would be stupid enough to send it to them, but there are a lot of greedy and dishonest people (it isn't their money even if it was real). Billions—not millions—*billions* of dollars have been lost in this scam by people who were greedy, dumb and a little dishonest.

Never give or lend money to someone you don't know. (Even if you lend to people you do know, you often won't get it back. That includes relatives. Trust me on this.). Never give out personal information, like a credit card number or social security number to someone who contacts you by phone or text or e-mail. Chances are it's a scam, and they want to rob you or steal your identity and run up bills in your name. Often they pretend to be your bank or the government. Be sure to keep your check book in a safe place. Evil people like to get your checks and forge your name so they can steal your money.

The scam thieves take advantage of the greedy and dishonest. But they also take advantage of the gullible and kind-hearted. You are not greedy or dishonest, and we hope you never will be. You are kind-hearted, and we hope you will stay that way—but not be gullible so bad people can take advantage of you and hurt you.

You shouldn't spoil your life by never trusting anyone. But neither should you put yourself at risk by being careless or gullible.

Drugs, Alcohol and Smoking

Adults talk and talk and talk to kids about drugs. And, year after year kids don't listen. Of course, a lot of adults, having dived into the drug cesspool when they were young, choose to live the sad life of a druggie and never get out. Worse, some get out—then dive right back in!

Some people think it's because many people have such sad, poor lives, they want drugs to dull their senses, to take them away from reality. But there are any number of rich and famous people who have ruined—or ended—their lives by abusing drugs. I don't know how to explain someone who had everything the world could offer choosing a behavior that kills them before they are thirty years old.

Look at the rich and famous rock stars who killed themselves at a young age by getting into drugs. The rock singer Janis Joplin had it made when she died of a heroin overdose at age 27.

The rock singer Jimi Hendrix was rich and famous when he died, apparently of an over dose of sleeping pills, at age 27. Reports claim he smothered in his own vomit. Hendrix also was reported to use marijuana, LSD and other illegal drugs.

Jerry Garcia, the wealthy member of the ironically-named Grateful Dead rock group made it all the way to 53 years old, before he died in a drug rehab center of a heart attack, believed to be a result of his using illegal drugs.

Kurt Cobain was another famous rock star who died at 27, shooting himself under the influence of heroin. There are many others. In fact, wikipedia.org has a long list of drug-related deaths of celebrities.

Why? Why would someone who has everything a person could want use deadly drugs?

I think there are three reasons people abuse drugs. First, they have nothing they care about more than themselves. Druggies inflict a great deal of pain on their families, who see the sad way they live and, all too often, the sad way they die. To support their habits, they often steal from their parents, spouses and even children, because money from drugs comes way ahead of caring about the people who care about them. When they steal from their family to buy drugs, the message they send them is they care about getting high right now more than they ever cared about their loved ones.

Druggies are self-centered, not other-centered people.

Secondly, I think they are people whose brains lack the ability to visualize the future. They will do drugs to feel good right now even know they know it will ruin their lives in the future, because their brains aren't smart enough to imagine that a future will come. They will steal and lie today, even though it's obvious they will be found out tomorrow, because the concept of "tomorrow" is crowded out in their brains by what they want right now. Such people are usually bad at holding jobs or getting an education, because they don't get the idea of working hard now to have a better future.

Third, I think they think they are so "special" that, even though drugs ruin most people who abuse them, they think it won't affect them. This would explain the deaths of the young, famous people that I mentioned earlier. So many people fawn on them and tell them how wonderful they are, they think they can get high on drugs, with no bad consequences, because they are so special.

It's like thinking you are so special that you can step in front of a train without getting hurt. Of course, people don't do that, unless they want to die, because the bad result happens right now. The bad results of drug abuse, or alcohol abuse or smoking or other negative health behaviors happen in the future.

Young people are especially vulnerable to drugs because they tend to have the "I'm immortal" complex. They think they are young and healthy and will live forever—that bad things can't happen to them. Older people, who have more experience, know that bad things can and do happen. Which is why older people, who have fewer years to lose, are much more careful drivers than young people, with their whole lives to lose. Older people know that it can happen to you. They've seen it.

Unless they are rich from their families or being rock stars, there are only three ways to support a drug habit. Even if you have a great job, once you fry your brain on drugs, you won't keep it.

1. **Druggies can sell their bodies, if they are attractive enough, for sex**. That degrades them and destroys their self-image. They have to go through life knowing that everyone who knows them thinks of them as a whore. That's a bad word, and I'm sorry to have to use it, but it's important that you know how serious this is.

2. **They can steal**. This can give them a criminal record. It also means that no one who knows them will ever trust them again. People who steal from their families become outcasts within their families. I can promise you that no matter what, your Grandma and I will love you as long as we draw breath. But if you stole from us to buy drugs, we'd never fully trust you again. If you did it more than once, we wouldn't be able to trust you at all. One of the important bonds of family would be broken.

3. **They can become drug sellers, getting other people hooked and passing the poison on**. That's a nasty, evil thing to do. If I could push a button and all the drug dealers on Earth would vanish, they'd all be gone and the world would be a better place.

No one trusts them for another reason. They are also good liars. They have to be to cover up their drug usage and the things to do to pay for drugs. Even the people who love them can never trust them again.

You don't want to drag yourself in the gutter by doing any or all of the things necessary to support a drug habit.

People claim that drug abuse is a disease, like cancer or my pulmonary fibrosis, so drug abusers aren't responsible for their actions. It may have some characteristics of disease, but it's the only disease you can catch by deciding to do it. It's not like a giant germ runs out of an alley, grabs you and stuffs the drugs up your nose.

I think the "disease" excuse is too often a cop out, so that no one has to be personally responsible for the decisions they made to abuse drugs.

They say the same thing about alcohol abuse. So if I'm mad at someone, say for stealing from me, and I go out and have a few beers, then punch that person in the face, it wouldn't be my fault? We could blame it on the beer and everyone should forgive me? Even if I did it over and over?

Not everyone who uses illegal drugs completely destroys their lives. A few people recover from it, just as some alcoholics recover from abusing booze. Others use some milder illegal drug, like marijuana, and can go on functioning pretty well. But even with marijuana, many become potheads, unable to do well at work or school because they are spaced out. Then they figure they are fine, might as well try one of the harder drugs.

There's another reason not to use illegal drugs. Reports suggest that there have been over 50,000 murders in Mexico due to drug cartel killings in the last four years. A number of the dead, of course, are fellow drug-thugs, and no loss to the world. But many are innocent men, women and children just caught up in the violence. If it were not for illegal drug usage in the US, there would be no obscene drug profits to fight over, thus no drug war. Every drug abuser in America thus has the blood of innocent children on his or her hands.

How does someone get into drugs? They get asked by friends. I think few people wake up in the morning and say, "Wow, it's a great day. I think I'll become a pothead or a heroin addict today, start stealing from my family, lose my job, maybe die young. What could be more fun?"

Often they are with friends, perhaps at a party, and the friends try to talk them into it. Just as people drinking booze don't like to be around people who aren't—the spoil sports!—people doing drugs are uncomfortable doing them in front of people who aren't hooked and spaced out. Some people are weak and very subject to what's called "peer pressure." They will do things they don't want to because they think, wrongly, it will make them popular. The friends will lie and say you can't get hooked, just try it once. Then, because it does make you feel good, you try it just once more. Soon the drug owns you and your family.

Or sometimes the "friend" is a drug seller, or has a drug seller who wants more customers, so they want to get you hooked. In other cases, a boy will talk a girl into trying pot or other drugs (including alcohol), because he wants her to have sex with him, and thinks—often correctly—that being woozy-headed will make her more likely to give in. If she winds up pregnant he's not likely to be there to support the child. Nor will he help if she gets a nasty disease from the sex.

The rule is easy to say. Never do anything that makes you uncomfortable because other people want you to for their reasons. Do things only because you want to. (No, I'm not talking about going to a restaurant or a movie someone else likes. I'm talking about the serious things that can change or destroy your life.) I know it's a hard rule to follow.

The evidence is pretty clear. If you want to live a shorter, nasty, unhappy life, and have people look down on you, drugs are one of the best ways. Almost 40,000 Americans die every year from drug abuse. Don't be one of them.

Alcohol

Alcohol is also a drug. It happens to be a legal drug, at least for people over 21. A large part of the population enjoys alcohol. It is also the most widely abused drug and people get addicted to alcohol just as they do to other drugs. People who abuse alcohol also often ruin their lives and die younger. Alcoholism can run in families. I'm very lucky that I seem to have escaped the tendency, because my father and grandfather were alcoholics, but I monitor my drinking, because I don't want to ruin my life or Grandma's life and lose my job.

Alcohol results in tens of thousands of deaths every year in car crashes from people who drive after they have been drinking, because it slows their reflexes, distorts their vision and impairs their judgment. And many of the dead are not the drinkers, but those innocent people riding in cars either with the drinker, or that are hit by the drinker. Too many of them are children. I can't imagine anything worse than going through life knowing you killed a child because you were stupid enough to drive after a few drinks. Or that your child died because you let her ride with someone who had been drinking.

Teenagers are usually eager to try alcohol. Certainly your Grandfather was! So telling them not to drink usually doesn't work.

If you are going to try drinking, be very careful where, when and with who you drink. Alcohol not only impairs your judgment, but also your ability to protect yourself. Every year hundreds of girls get raped at parties, sometimes by a gang of boys they don't even know at a party. I'm told that's a pretty unpleasant experience that leaves a girl injured, feeling very bad about herself, and too often with a disease or unwanted baby. Finding yourself with AIDS or a child at 14, because you decided to have a few drinks with friends, isn't the route to a good life.

And if your friends are drinking too, you can't count on them to protect you.

Never make important decisions when you have been drinking, because drinking makes your judgment fly away. Important decisions would include having sex with a new partner, going for a ride with a drunk driver, getting a tattoo, trying drugs, starting smoking or joining the French Foreign Legion. Okay, joining the Legion is pretty unlikely, but the rest can turn a fun night into a life-destroyer.

When you are an adult having a few drinks in safe company and feeling mellow is one of the pleasures of life. Getting rip-roaring, commode-hugging drunk is not a lot of fun. It makes you do really stupid things and feel terrible for the next day, perhaps even for the next week. That, I'm sad to say, no one had to tell me. I learned from experience.

Also, you can get alcohol poisoning, and die, if you drink too much. Every year, some teens who think, "It can't happen to me," die from binge drinking, leaving their families with a wound that never heals.

Like a car or a gun, alcohol is a tool that can make life better—or destroy it. Be very careful with it. Some things you break can be fixed or replaced. If you drink and kill yourself or someone else, it can never be fixed. And, yes, it CAN happen to you.

Smoking

Smokers die younger, about ten years younger than non-smokers, on the average. About 435,000 people every year—the population of a small city—die from tobacco use. They suffer from more illness and disease. They smell bad. They start fires. They waste a lot of money on tobacco. Nicotine in tobacco is an addictive drug, just like heroin or alcohol.

About one out of every hundred non-smokers dies of lung cancer. But one out of every four smokers does. Lung cancer is a terrible way to die. Smoking also causes emphysema (which killed my dad) where you smother or your heart gives out because it doesn't get enough oxygen. It causes other kinds of cancer and other diseases, like heart disease. *Smoking kills.* Period.

Because it is so bad for you, people look at smokers and think how dumb they are. Do you want people to think you are dumb? Start smoking.

Just being around smokers increases your risk of diseases of the lungs and heart from second-hand smoke. Kids whose parents smoke are sicker more often than kids who live in non-smoking families, and more likely to smoke themselves.

So why is anyone dumb enough to start smoking? Once again, peer pressure. The other kids tell you that you aren't cool, aren't "mature" if you don't smoke like they do. The pressure to conform can get pretty intense.

Both my best friends in high school smoked cigarettes. And they teased and insulted me pretty hard because I didn't. It's what kids do.

In response, I started smoking a pipe. Because I didn't inhale it, my risk of lung cancer wasn't a lot higher than just being around smokers, and I didn't get addicted to nicotine, so many years ago, when I decided the risk of mouth and throat cancer were too great, I was able to quit without problems. Maybe because I didn't smoke it that often. But you know what, when I see a pipe at a flea market, I still wish I could smoke it. That would be pretty dumb to do, even though the doctors don't think my lung disease, pulmonary fibrosis, is related to smoking.

When someone smokes around you, they are putting poison in *your* body. Nothing says, "I don't care about you as much as I care about my own enjoyment" like a parent smoking with a child in the car or in the house.

Because we love you so much, Grandma and I ask you, *please* don't do illegal drugs, *please* don't smoke and *please* use alcohol only in moderation, if at all, when you are an adult. All three can make you a slave. We want you to be free, healthy and happy. And to live a long life.

Tattoos and Piercings

I want you to go to your closet and pick out your favorite top. The one you love best for color, design and fit. Got it? Okay now put it on. And wear it for the rest of your life. Sure, as you get older, it will stretch out of shape, but who cares? It's your favorite now, so it will be your favorite every day for the rest of your life, right? You can wash it, of course, but put it right back on—or wear it in the shower and wash it there. It will fade, and styles will change, but since it's your favorite now, it's be your favorite in fifty years, won't it? Especially after looking at it every day.

If that sounds silly, how come so many people get tattoos? It's a design they like now, so they think that they will always like it. Even when they get old and wrinkly, and it fades and stretches, they will still want to wear it every day. Or so I guess they believe.

When your Grandma and I were kids, you might give advice to a boy about tattoos, but I bet no one talked to her about them. Tattoos were something that rough men—sailors, Marines, dock workers and criminals—got. Twenty years ago, studies showed that a man with a tattoo was much more likely to commit a serious crime than one without one. Though I'm a Marine, I don't have any tattoos. I was rarely tempted, as I knew they were permanent, and I figured if I didn't like it in a few years, I'd be stuck.

Now, with lasers, tattoos can be removed, or at least faded. Usually there is a lingering discoloration and perhaps scarring. And I read that it is also expensive and somewhat painful. Some doctors who make good money removing tattoos estimate that about half the people who get tattoos later regret them. That's not great odds. Of course, it depends on the tattoo. Doctors say that the most-often removed tattoo is the name of a former boyfriend or girlfriend, after the relationship has ended, as relationships often do. Your Grandma's name is Bonnie. If I had the name of an old girlfriend named Mary tattooed on my arm, how do you think she would feel about looking at it every day?

Unless they were low-class guttersnipes, like prostitutes, tarts and gang girls, girls didn't get tattoos when Grandma and I were young. That's all changed in the last few years, as more and more perfectly-respectable young women choose to put permanent designs on their bodies.

You can tell I don't much like tattoos, especially on girls. I think God made you perfect, and getting a tattoo is like drawing on a great work of art with a magic marker, expecting it to look better when you are finished. I think tattoos make a girl less attractive, not more attractive.

And some people, men and women, go in for a lot of tattoos, or huge tattoos over large parts of their bodies. That's even uglier. There's a big difference between a small rose or butterfly on a girl's hip, and a tattoo of a snake that curls around her neck and slithers up her face over her nose!

Because lots of people still think of tattoos as something that only low-class or criminal people have, the man—or especially the woman—with visible tattoos on the face, neck, arms or hands often loses out on the good jobs. Sometimes they lose out on love, because a person of high status may not date them because of the tattoos.

Piercings have similar problems, though a lot of them will heal once taken out. Unless they leave ugly scars, especially if they get infected. I'm fine with pierced ears, though I think multiple piercings look dumb, or like a person from a primitive tribe. And because every piercing creates the risk of infection, I personally wouldn't take the risk of having a very young girl's ears pierced until she was old enough to decide if she wanted it done. Often doing so is more about the mother's vanity and ego, since the baby doesn't know any difference.

I even think that a pierced belly button on a young girl who has a flat belly can look cute. And, again, it can be taken out and heal. But she'd be better off without it.

Face and especially tongue piercings make me want to throw up. Like tattoos, they open up routes where infection and disease can enter the body. With tongue piercings, they create a permanent wound in a place that is full of germs. It's like cutting your finger and sticking it in the toilet. Before you flush. And leaving it there. Yuck.

So my best advice is not to get a piercing or tattoo, not even, "I love Grandpa" on your back. Not many people regret the tattoos they didn't get, but a lot regret the ones they have to look at every day, especially when they get older.

Never get a tattoo or a piercing because a boyfriend or a girlfriend wants you to. Doing something risky and permanent should only be because you want to, and have thought long and carefully about it. Never get one if you have been drinking or your judgment is impaired in any way. What seems like a good idea when you are partying may seem very sad when you wake up the next day.

But if you join the Marines and serve with honor for four years, I'll say okay to a tattoo of a very small Marine Corps Emblem. Where no one can see it. And only if you really want it!

Sex, Boys and Dating

Since you are all of eleven years old as I write this, there could hardly be a topic designed to make a grandfather more uncomfortable. But I still have to write about it, because you are starting to become aware of sex and because the pressures in our society are encouraging many kids to have sex at a younger age.

Also, I'm hoping you will reread this book as you get into your teens and young adulthood, and find it of increasing value.

You'll notice from the title I'm assuming that like the majority of girls, you will like boys. If you turn out to be one of those girls who prefers girls—it's hard to tell at this age—your Grandma and I will still love you every bit as much and still want you to be happy with your choices and your life. But, since my own preference has always been for the opposite sex, I can not give you some of the advice you'd need in that case. However, some of my advice here will still apply.

I can say "Don't smoke," and "Don't do drugs," with some hope that you will agree and never try either one. It's a lot harder to "just say no" to sex. Every biological and emotional drive in teens and young adults—not to mention what they see on TV and the Internet and hear from friends—pushes them towards having sex. That drive is why the human race has survived and why there are almost seven billion people on Earth. Or so they tell me—I haven't counted.

Sexual relations with someone you care about can be wonderful. The old joke goes that sex isn't the only thing in life, but it sure beats whatever is in second place.

But sex can also create untold misery and evil, when used carelessly or too casually. Careless sex can lead to bringing a child into the world before you are equipped to support or care for her. It can lead to nasty diseases, some of which, like AIDS, you can die from. It can be used to degrade you and destroy your reputation.

It is a curious fact that the boy who was so insistent on you having sex one day, will often speak bad of you to other boys, who will tell other girls, in the days after you give in. It always seemed to me that if the girl was wrong to have sex, so was the boy, but you rarely hear boys called bad names like "slut" for having sex. We might wish the culture was different, and it has changed a lot since Grandma and I were young, but girls are still viewed differently than boys about sex.

You should never have sex because someone else wants you to for his pleasure. Having sex doesn't prove you love someone, and if he loved you, he wouldn't pressure you.

Teenage boys rarely have the best interests of the girl at heart when it comes to sex. In fact, they really have no understanding of their own long-term best interests, never mind the girl's best interests. Trust me on this—I was a teenage boy. Just last week, if I remember correctly.

The back seat of a car, when you are excited, is not the best time or location to decide about having sex. And it's hard not to decide to "go all the way," once you've gone a certain distance. It's also much harder to say "no" when your judgment has been impaired by booze or drugs—which is why boys will also try to talk you into drinking or taking drugs.

Also, thousands of girls are "date-raped" ever year by boys who were perfectly nice—but changed under the influence of sexual drive, and forced them. Others go to parties and are raped by strange boys. That would be a pretty unpleasant experience, and could do permanent psychological or physical damage.

Many girls seem to like "bad boys," the wild kids who like to party, drink, have sex and perhaps do drugs. These boys are often very popular—more so than the quiet "boring" kid who studies and doesn't ruin his future by getting in trouble. But in ten or fifteen years, these "boring" boys will be men, taking care of their kids, earning a good living at a good job and supporting their families. The fun "bad boys" often leave heartsick single mothers living in poverty and misery behind them. But they are popular and fun at the time. Unfortunately, most teen girls aren't able to see that far in the future and make good decisions about who to hang out with.

I don't want to stop you from having fun. But I do want you to protect yourself by avoiding situations where you are not in control of what happens.

If you do reach a point where you decide to have sex, hopefully in a long term, loving relationship that has a future, always use protection against having children or getting a disease until you are married and can afford to support kids. Single mothers usually live hard lives in poverty and their kids do as well.

So, having given you this advice about sex that you didn't ask for, you are entitled to ask, "Grandpa, if someone would have told you all this when you were 16, would you have listened?"

The answer is no. But my job here, as a very old, experienced and maybe even a bit wise person who loves you, is to give you the best advice for having a happy life that I can. And at least, when I started having sex at age 17, I was careful never to bring a child I couldn't support into the world. I hope you will do even better, and be even happier than I have been.

Oh, and if you have any more questions about sex? Ask Grandma.

Voting

Voting for who you want to run the government is an important responsibility of every citizen. Since I came back from Vietnam and was then old enough to vote (it was 21 then), I've hardly ever missed an election or a primary.

There are always campaigns to get more people to vote. But I don't agree. What I want are efforts to get more people to vote intelligently and responsibly.

People who vote stupidly produce bad public officials. When I was a State Senator, we used to call the dumb voters the "donkey vote."

Who are the donkey voters?

Well, political scientists say that for the lower offices (those below President, Governor or US Senator, which would include the office of state senator) having your name first on the ballot is usually worth 5% of the vote. If that's true, it means that one person out of every 20 picks their elected officials by how the ballot is arranged! How dumb is that?

Many people vote only for members of one party or the other. It's true that party membership can give you some idea of where a candidate stands on a lot of issues, but it tells you nothing about a candidate's ability or character. Anyone can belong to either party. So if Mr. Jones runs as a Republican this year and a Democrat in two years, they vote for him one time and against him the other time, even though he is the same person.

I consider myself a member of a party, but if a crook runs for office as a member of my party, I don't have to vote for him. And I don't.

Many people vote for candidates because they are the same race, or gender, or religion or ethnic group as they are. How dumb is that? Being a man or a woman, of Irish or Italian or Hispanic or African or Chinese heritage doesn't make you the better or the worse person. Neither can you know that because one candidate is a woman and the other is a man, one is better than the other. Because one candidate goes to a Catholic church, another goes to a Jewish temple and a third doesn't go at all doesn't tell you who is the best person to hold office.

I think there are three things you should consider in deciding who to vote for.

The first is *character*. Is the person honest? Does he or she have moral courage (the courage to take unpopular stands if they are right)? Is the candidate truthful. All of these fall under having integrity. It's important for you to have integrity. It's also vital for those elected to govern us to have it.

The second is *ability*. It the candidate smart? Does he or she have a good personality, thus the ability to work well with other officials to get things done? Is the candidate a good speaker and writer? Being able to communicate your positions to others is important in governing. Does the candidate have experience that will help him or her do a good job? No candidate has experience in every area the government deals with, but having some experience in the real world, dealing with real problems, helps.

The third is *issues*. Is the candidate in favor of many of the things you are in favor of and against many of the things you are against? (You can never find a candidate who agrees with you on everything. Even if you run for office yourself, you will find you cannot be sure about many issues.)

Looking for these three things in candidates makes voting decisions very hard. One candidate might be better on the issues, another have better ability and it's often hard to tell who has integrity! (But I would never vote for a candidate I didn't think had integrity, regardless of his ability or her position on the issues. We don't need more crooks in government.)

Trying to figure out who is the best candidate is hard work. You have to pay attention to the news, to what the candidates are saying, and to what other people are saying about them. You have to figure out where those other people are on the issues so you know if you can trust them. All of this takes time and concentration and effort. Which is why so many voters find it easy to be donkey voters, and pick their candidates by things that don't really matter.

I hope you'll be an informed, intelligent voter. But if you are too lazy to be a good citizen, it's better to stay home than be a donkey voter.

Words

In the book *Through the Looking Glass*, Humpty Dumpty says to Alice, "When **I** use a word, it means just what I choose it to mean — neither more nor less." The author, Lewis Carroll, was making a good point in a funny way. One of the confusing things about language is that people use the same words, but mean different things by them.

Politicians are experts at using words that mean different things to different people, because they want to get everyone's vote.

An example would be "fair." Everybody wants things to be fair, but everybody has a different idea of what fair is.

If I gave you one scoop of ice cream and your friend two scoops, you would probably say that wasn't fair. But suppose I hired you and your friend to cut my lawn. You work two hours and your friend works only one hour. Is it fair to pay you twice as much as the other person, or to be "fair" should I pay you both the same amount. After all, if you work twice as long and get twice as much money, you can buy twice as much ice cream. Is that fair?

Suppose you are a better worker, and though you each work only an hour, you cut twice as much grass as your friend. Should you get paid twice as much for cutting twice as much grass, or should you get paid the same because you worked the same amount of time? Each of you might mean something different when you said what was fair!

You know that I'm a bad singer. Really bad. And you know that some people get paid a lot of money to sing on TV. Wouldn't it be "fair" that I should also be paid for singing on TV, because after all, it isn't my fault that I'm a bad singer? And I should get paid as much as people who play sports, though even when I was young I wasn't a very good baseball or football player. Would that be fair? Or would it be fair that everyone can earn as much money as they can get someone to pay them for their work in what we call "the free market"? That way, one person gets to say how much he thinks is fair to pay for something, and the other person gets to decide if he is willing to work for that much money.

"Fair" means different things to different people. And nothing can ever be completely "fair" between two people, because everyone is different, and every situation is different. People who try to make things "fair" usually make them very unfair in other ways.

"Justice" is another word that means different things to different people. I may not think it's "fair" that some people have a lot more money than me, no matter if they earned it or won it or were given it. So I may demand "justice" so that some money they earned is taken from them and given to me. Of course, if I just took it myself, it would be called "stealing," not "justice"!

There are a lot of words in addition to "fair" and "justice" which sound good, but can be made to mean almost anything. Words like "free," "freedom," "hope," "love" and "change" may sound good—but you need to understand what the speaker means before you buy in.

Take "love." When I say I love coffee, I love books and I love you, I mean different things in each case. And I'm not even trying to fool anyone.

A boy may tell a girl that he "loves" her. What she may hear is that he cares for her more than any other girl, that he always wants to be with her, and that one day they will get married, have kids and live together forever. What he may really mean is that he likes her a lot tonight and wants to play kissy-face, cuddle-bear right now—but may be too busy to see her tomorrow.

We call words like "love" *emotion-laden* words, as they have a lot of emotion in them. Especially when someone wants you to do something, think about that person's words carefully. What does the speaker want you to think the words mean? And what do they really mean to the speaker?

People can be talked into silly, destructive or dangerous things very easily by good-sounding words.

As an experiment, a group of students at a college went around with a petition to ban the chemical di-hydrogen-oxide. They had a lot of good reasons. Di-hydrogen-oxide kills many people every year, it ruins homes and cars and can be very dangerous. Plus it was now in all our lakes and rivers, even in our drinking water. In fact, it was found in the bottled water you buy in the store, in coffee, tea and soda. All this is true.

So hundreds of students signed the petition to ban di-hydrogen-oxide. Which is a way to say H_2O. As you learned in school, that's the chemical formula for water. So all these smart college students were signing a petition to outlaw water. All because the words sounded good.

Words are wonderful things. Like you I love to read, and write and talk, none of which we could do without words.

But words are also something we need to be careful of. Like any other tool, they can be misused to do harmful things.

The Wisdom of Others

I've always thought that the way to be smarter was to read books by people smarter than I am, like the brilliant economist Dr. Thomas Sowell.

I've also collected hundreds of quotations from people who I thought were smart. Some I've used in the chapters above. Below are some other great ones. Their words of wisdom helped me have a successful life, and I hope they will help you as well. (But be warned. Sometimes people make up quotes and put famous people's names on them. I think all these are real.)

Some of these you won't understand until you think about them, or have more experience. Some are from famous people, others not so much. But I hope you will re-read them from time to time.

The world cares very little about what a man or woman knows; it is what a man or woman is able to do that counts. –Booker T. Washington

The darkest day of any man's life is when he sits down to plan how to get money without earning it. –Horace Greeley

While one person hesitates because he feels inferior, another is busy making mistakes and becoming superior. –Henry C. Link

A man who makes $100 a day and spends $99 will be rich. A man who makes $1000 a day and spends $1,001 will be poor. –Chit Ranawat, MD

Risk more than others think is safe. Care more than others think is wise. Dream more than others think is practical. Expect more than others think is possible. –Thomas Claude Bissell

Where parents do too much for their children, the children will not do much for themselves. –Elbert Hubbard

We must all suffer one of two things: the pain of discipline or the pain of regret and disappointment. –Jim Rohn

The world is full of willing people, some willing to work, the rest willing to let them. –Robert Frost

I'm a great believer in luck, and I find the harder I work the more I have of it. –Thomas Jefferson

If we wait for the moment when everything, absolutely everything is ready, we shall never begin. –Ivan Turgenev

Do more than you are paid for. There are never any traffic jams on the extra mile. –Brian Tracy

Never doubt that a small group of thoughtful committed citizens can change the world; indeed it's the only thing that ever has. –Margaret Mead

In any ethical situation, the thing you want least to do is probably the right action. –Jerry Pournelle

A man wrapped up in himself is a very small bundle. –Benjamin Franklin

Whoever renders service to many puts himself in line for greatness - great wealth, great return, great satisfaction, great reputation, and great joy. –Jim Rohn

Whenever good and evil compromise, evil always wins. –Ayn Rand

If we encounter a man of rare intellect, we should ask him what books he reads. –Ralph Waldo Emerson

Nothing strengthens the judgment and quickens the conscience like individual responsibility. –Elizabeth Cady Stanton

It's not whether you get knocked down, it's whether you get up. –Vince Lombardi

What is left when honor is lost? –Publilius Syrus

Do what you love and you'll never have to work again. –Chinese Proverb

Fame is vapor, popularity an accident, riches take wing. Only one thing endures and that is character. –Abraham Lincoln

Never give in, never give in, never, never, never - in nothing, great or small, large or petty - never give in except to convictions of honor and good sense –Winston Churchill

Most folks are about as happy as they make up their minds to be.

–Abraham Lincoln

The world is a dangerous place, not because of those who do evil, but because of those who look on and do nothing. –Albert Einstein

Broadly speaking, short words are best, and the old words, when short, are the best of all –Winston Churchill.

Half the harm that is done in this world is due to people who want to feel important. They don't mean to do harm – but the harm does not interest them. Or they do not see it, or they justify it because they are absorbed in the endless struggle to think well of themselves. –T.S. Eliot

Determine never to be idle. No person will have occasion to complain of the want of time, who never loses any. It is wonderful how much may be done, if we are always doing. –Thomas Jefferson

Be kind, for everyone you meet is fighting a hard battle. –Plato

Experience keeps a dear school, but fools will learn in no other. --Benjamin Franklin ("dear" means expensive).

The man with a new idea is a crank until the idea succeeds. –Mark Twain

There is nothing more difficult to take in hand, more perilous to conduct, or more uncertain in its success, than to take the lead in the introduction of a new order of things. —Machiavelli

Avoiding danger is no safer in the long run than outright exposure. The fearful are caught as often as the bold. —Helen Keller

Those who deny freedom to others, deserve it not for themselves; and, under a just God, cannot long retain it. —Abraham Lincoln

In the end more than they wanted freedom, they wanted security. When the Athenians finally wanted not to give to society but for society to give to them, when the freedom they wished for was freedom from responsibility, then Athens ceased to be free and was never free again —Edward Gibbon

One of the penalties for refusing to participate in politics is that you end up being governed by your inferiors. —Plato

Labor to keep alive in your breast that little spark of celestial fire called conscience. —George Washington

Just because you do not take an interest in politics doesn't mean politics won't take an interest in you. —Pericles

A positive attitude may not solve all your problems, but it will annoy enough people to make it worth the effort. —Herm Albright

Surround yourself with the best people you can find, delegate authority, and don't interfere. —Ronald Reagan

I don't think much of a man who is not wiser today than he was yesterday. –Abraham Lincoln

I cannot give the formula for success, but I can give you the formula of failure - which is try to please everybody. –Herbert B. Swope

There is no safety for honest men except by believing all possible evil of evil men. –Edmund Burke

Drive carefully - Better to be ten minutes late in this world, than ten years early in the next! –Adele MacGregor-Blain

Final Thoughts

Your greatest asset is that you care about and love others.

Before you do something, think. If you'd be ashamed to have everyone know you did it, then you probably shouldn't do it.

If the most important thing in your life is what you see in the mirror in the morning, I can say with a fair amount of certitude that you will have an unhappy life.

Things will always be crazy around you. That's life. You need to learn how to focus and rise above it, to live happy so it doesn't make you crazy too.

Always look for mentors, people who can teach you, lead you and set a shining example for you. Avoid negative people, or people who lie and steal from others. They will wreck your life if you allow them too close.

Likewise, you should live so that you can be a role model to others and a mentor for many. It is very satisfying to help others along this rocky road we call life.

Contentment won't come from how much you have. A little will come from what you've accomplished. But most will come from how much you have cared for and helped other people.

Try to live without regret. You will make mistakes. Perfection isn't possible. But constant improvement is.

Don't judge people by what they say, but by what they do.

Education is not something a person achieves. It is a process that a person engages in throughout life. In my view, anyone who doesn't read 12 to 20 serious, non-fiction books a year in subjects like politics, history, economics, current events, and biography, among others, cannot claim to be educated. Reading to stay current in your job doesn't count.

The most powerful words in the world are, "I'm sorry. I was wrong. I'll fix it and try to do better in the future." They are hard to say, but they can repair a lot of damage. The person who always tries to blame mistakes on other people or events is never respected or liked.

I fear that our country is headed for bad times. There seems to be something in human nature that when things are good for a lot of people, greed and envy rise and short-sighted people over-turn the apple cart. The best way to face the future and deal with bad times is to be well-educated and have many useful skills. To have a network of people you can depend on and who can depend on you. To have few debts and live simply. Debt makes you a slave to others. Having a lot doesn't make you happy, but it does make you a target. If your life is simple and you are not loaded down with "stuff" (like your Grandma and I are!), you can be flexible and move easily if you have to.

One last thing darling girl. Love never dies. Even when I'm gone, and your Grandma is gone, we will still love you. In fact, I'll love you more!

Made in the USA
Charleston, SC
17 February 2012